CAMPAIGN 384

JAPANESE CONQUEST OF BURMA 1942

The Advance to the Gates of India

TIM MOREMAN

ILLUSTRATED BY JOHNNY SHUMATE

Series editor Nikolai Bogdanovic

OSPREY PUBLISHING
Bloomsbury Publishing Plc
Kemp House, Chawley Park, Cumnor Hill, Oxford OX2 9PH, UK
29 Earlsfort Terrace, Dublin 2, Ireland
1385 Broadway, 5th Floor, New York, NY 10018, USA
E-mail: info@ospreypublishing.com
www.ospreypublishing.com

OSPREY is a trademark of Osprey Publishing Ltd

First published in Great Britain in 2022

A catalogue record for this book is available from the British Library.

ISBN: PB 9781472849731; eBook 9781472849724; ePDF 9781472849755;
XML 9781472849748

22 23 24 25 26   10 9 8 7 6 5 4 3 2 1

Maps by Bounford.com
3D BEVs by Paul Kime
Index by Rob Munro
Typeset by PDQ Digital Media Solutions, Bungay, UK
Printed and bound in India by Replika Press Private Ltd.

Artist's note

Readers can discover more about the work of illustrator Johnny Shumate at
the below website:

https://johnnyshumate.com

Osprey Publishing supports the Woodland Trust, the UK's leading woodland
conservation charity.

To find out more about our authors and books visit
www.ospreypublishing.com. Here you will find extracts, author
interviews, details of forthcoming events and the option to sign up for
our newsletter.

A note on unit abbreviations

In this work, battalions of regiments are referred to using Roman numerals,
e.g. II./7th Gurkha Rifles (2nd Battalion, 7th Gurkha Rifle Regiment).
Companies within regiments are referred to using Arabic numerals,
e.g. 2./II./7th Gurkha Rifles (2nd Company of 2nd Battalion, 7th Gurkha
Rifle Regiment).

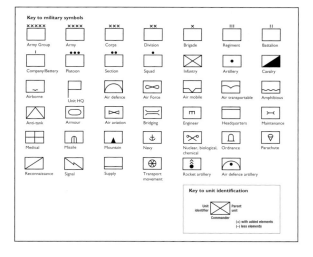

Front cover main illustration: On 7 March 1942, Japanese infantry
defend a hastily improvised roadblock on the Prome road, Taukkyan,
from an Allied Bren Gun carrier accompanied by troops of the
1st Gloucesters. (Johnny Shumate)

Title page photograph: Japanese troops led by an officer
brandishing a sword advance through clouds of smoke and dust
towards the city of Mandalay. (adoc-photos/Corbis via Getty Images)

CONTENTS

Burma and South-East Asia, early 1942

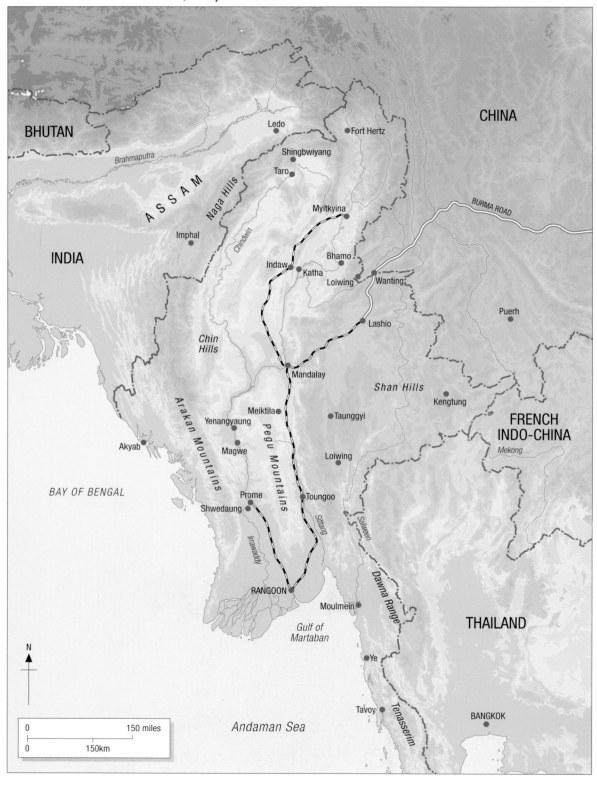

BHUTAN

CHINA

Brahmaputra

Ledo

Fort Hertz

Shingbwiyang

A S S A M

Taro

Naga Hills

Myitkyina

BURMA ROAD

Imphal

Chindwin

INDIA

Indaw

Bhamo

Katha

Loiwing

Wanting

Puerh

Chin
Hills

Lashio

Mandalay

Shan Hills

Meiktila

Kengtung

Yenangyaung

Taunggyi

FRENCH
INDO-CHINA

Akyab

Magwe

Arakan Mountains

Pegu Mountains

Loiwing

Mekong

BAY OF BENGAL

Prome

Toungoo

Shwedaung

Sittang

Irrawaddy

Salween

Dawna Range

THAILAND

RANGOON

Moulmein

Gulf of
Martaban

N

Ye

BANGKOK

Tavoy

Tenasserim

Andaman Sea

0   150 miles

0   150km

ORIGINS OF THE CAMPAIGN

The British colony of Burma, a vast and stunningly beautiful country the size of France and Belgium combined, was a military backwater before September 1939, with the newly constructed naval base at Singapore – built to home a Royal Navy battle fleet despatched from European waters in event of war – occupying centre stage in wider imperial defence strategy in the Far East. Since the annexation of Burma, a diverse agricultural country consisting of wide-open plains in its centre fringed by high jungle-covered mountains, to British India on 1 January 1886, maintaining internal security was the primary concern of the imperial authorities. During the inter-war period keeping the peace amongst its sometimes-unruly Burmese population was the task of just two undermanned and poorly equipped British infantry battalions and a single locally raised infantry regiment – the four-battalion-strong Burma Rifles recruited from a handful of Burmese and Gurkhas, Karens, Chins and Kachins. A mountain artillery battery and a field company of sappers 'on loan' from India Command rounded off the tiny garrison. These regular units were complemented by the tiny part-time Burma Auxiliary Force, recruited from Europeans, Anglo-Burmese and Anglo-Indians. Locally raised paramilitaries – three battalions of Burma Military

Burmese troops man a .303 Vickers medium machine gun during training deep in the jungle in August 1941. (AirSeaLand)

A battery of Indian mountain artillery, equipped with 3.7in. howitzers, carried broken down in constituent parts on mules, is seen on the march among the Shan Hills, Burma, in December 1941. (AP/Shutterstock)

Police and six battalions of the Burma Frontier Force – under civil control shouldered responsibility for maintaining law and order – 'watch and ward' – amongst the fractious tribes inhabiting the mountainous, jungle-covered tracts around its periphery.

China and Siam (Thailand) – the only potentially hostile countries sharing a land border with Burma – posed a distant and highly unlikely external threat to imperial rule, given the extreme difficulty of crossing the jungle-clad mountain ranges lying between them and Burma, across which roads and railways were marked by their near complete absence. The warships of the Royal Navy patrolling the Indian Ocean provided Burma's shield from seaborne invasion by a Great Power. Little changed after Burma became administratively a separate colony from India in April 1937 and the Burmese were given a legislature of their own in a grudging nod to self-government. Although a Burmese Prime Minister and cabinet governed the country, defence and foreign affairs remained firmly the responsibility of a British governor, with a newly formed defence department at Rangoon funded by local taxation overseeing a garrison that in reality remained heavily dependent on India for defence.

The outbreak of World War II in Europe in September 1939 had little direct impact on everyday life in Burma or its defence, with its airfields at Akyab, Mingaladon near Rangoon and Victoria Point – stepping-stones on the air reinforcement route to British colonies further east – arguably providing its only direct military contribution to wider imperial defence. War remained distant and remote. Although the despatch of a large battle fleet to Singapore became increasingly unlikely given the deteriorating situation in home

The Burma Road, used to carry weapons, ammunition, fuel and other vital war materials by lorry to Yunnan, provided a vital lifeline for Nationalist China. (Keystone/Getty Images)

waters and the Mediterranean in 1940–41, a dwindling flotilla of Royal Navy warships still shielded Burma in the Bay of Bengal from a seaborne invasion. Indeed, the colony's greatest contribution to the war effort lay in providing vitally needed rice (Burma was the 'rice basket' of South-East Asia), timber, oil and scarce wolfram.

The strategic significance of the colony gradually increased during the early war years, with a palpable Japanese 'threat' to Burmese security steadily emerging. Following the Japanese occupation of northern Indo-China in September 1940, Burma's strategic significance became even greater as the Burma Road (completed in 1939) provided embattled Nationalist China's only link to the outside world, now that Imperial Japan had sealed all other routes. This truly impressive 717-mile-long feat of civil engineering allowed vitally needed stocks of US arms, ammunition and other war materials, landed at Rangoon and then shipped by rail to Lashio, to be transported across the mountains aboard Lend Lease lorries, to reach China and keep the Nationalist armies fighting. The increasing open bellicosity of Imperial Japan – it repeatedly demanded the closure of the Burma Road, joined the Axis pact on 27 July 1940 and then on 13 April 1941 signed a neutrality pact with Nazi Germany and Soviet Russia – caused growing consternation amongst defence planners in the UK, Malaya and Burma. Following the unexpected outbreak of war between the USSR and Nazi Germany on 22 June 1941, Japan acted, and in early August 1941 it occupied southern Indo-China, giving it access to Vichy French airfields and naval bases. This act brought Malaya and Burma within range of Japanese aircraft, as well as increasing the possibility of an overland invasion of Burma via Laos and Siam. A review carried out by the Chiefs of Staff in August 1941 concluded Imperial Japan could now launch air raids on Burma in the event of war, but still discounted an overland invasion via Thailand through the Shan States as unlikely, as long as Malaya remained securely in British hands. The Singapore naval base and the large military garrison in Malaya and on Singapore Island still remained the primary defensive shield, which would have to be overcome before colonial Burma and India were threatened by a large-scale attack. Not only was a Japanese 'threat' discounted, a deadly combination of hubris, stupidity and pig-headed ignorance meant British senior commanders greatly underestimated the fighting ability of Imperial Japan's armed forces, despite growing evidence from China to the contrary.

This contribution to the Osprey Campaign series charts the ensuing Japanese invasion of Burma that began in December 1941 and ended in May 1942, following Burma Army's defeat on the battlefield in southern Burma and the ensuing 3½-month, 1,000-mile-long Allied fighting retreat from Rangoon northwards to safety in British India.

Japanese troops serving in Fifteenth Army assembled on a mountainside salute the rising sun shortly before the beginning of the Japanese invasion of Burma. (Vintage Space/Alamy)

CHRONOLOGY

1941

8 December
The Japanese Twenty-Fifth Army invades Thailand and northern Malaya.

12 December
Japanese troops cross the border into southern Burma and later seize the airfield at Victoria Point.

23 December
The Japanese 5th Air Division bombs Rangoon and Mingaladon airfield for the first time.

27 December
Lieutenant-General Tom Hutton assumes command of Burma Army, replacing Major-General Donald McLeod.

29 December
General Sir Archibald Wavell appointed Supreme Commander of Australian, British, Dutch and American Command (ABDACOM).

31 December
The 8th Indian Heavy Anti-Aircraft Battery and 3rd Indian Light Anti-Aircraft Battery land at Rangoon.

1942

1 January
Air Vice Marshal Donald Stevenson assumes command of the Royal Air Force in Burma – No. 221 Group, RAF Burma.

9 January
Major-General J.G. Smyth and the Headquarters of 17th Indian Division land at Rangoon. He takes command of British Commonwealth troops already deployed in Tenasserim.

16 January
46th Indian Infantry Brigade lands at Rangoon.

19 January
Japanese troops capture the airfield and town of Tavoy in Tenasserim.

20–23 January
The town of Mergui is evacuated.

20 January
The Japanese Fifteenth Army's leading formation – 55th Division – crosses the frontier into Burma at Myaaddy and Pauk, followed by 33rd Division.

20–22 January
16th Indian Infantry Brigade is badly defeated at Kawkareik.

30–31 January
The coastal town of Moulmein is captured by the Japanese 55th Division.

31 January
The 48th Indian Infantry Brigade lands at Rangoon.

8–9 February
The Japanese 143rd Regiment crosses the River Salween at Hmawbi.

10–11 February
The Japanese 33rd Division crosses the River Salween near Kuzeik, where the VII./10th Baluch Regiment is virtually destroyed in fierce fighting.

15 February
The 17th Indian Division concentrates to fight behind the Bilin River.

Malaya Command surrenders to the Japanese Twenty-Fifth Army at Singapore.

16–20 February
The Battle of the Bilin River.

19 February
The HQ of 17th Indian Division orders a withdrawal from the Bilin River.

21 February
The 7th Armoured Brigade and 1st Battalion, Queen's Own Cameron Highlanders land at Rangoon.

22–23 February
The Sittang Bridge is blown up to deny it to the Japanese – leaving two brigades behind on the eastern bank – effectively destroying 17th Indian Division as a fighting formation.

22 February
ABDACOM is dissolved. Wavell becomes commander-in-chief in India.

25–26 February
Heavy Japanese air raids on Rangoon.

27 February	The Japanese begin infiltrating across the Sittang River.
28 February	General Sir Archibald Wavell resumes his post as commander-in-chief in India.
1 March	Major-General J.G. Smyth is sacked as General Officer Commanding (GOC) 17th Indian Division and replaced by Major-General David 'Punch' Cowan.
	The Governor of Burma leaves Rangoon for Maymyo.
3 March	The Japanese cross the Sittang River in strength and advance towards Rangoon.
	1st Indian Field Regiment, equipped with 25pdr field artillery, lands at Rangoon.
*c.***4 March**	63rd Indian Infantry Brigade lands at Rangoon.
5 March	General Sir Harold Alexander assumes command of Burma Army.
7 March	The escape of the Rangoon garrison. 17th Indian Division and 7th Armoured Brigade are held up at Taukkyan by a Japanese roadblock.
8 March	The Japanese 33rd Division captures Rangoon, isolating Burma Army and cutting the Burma Road.
	The Chinese 200th Division relieves 1st Burma Division at Toungoo, with the latter redeploying to the Sittang Valley.

The docks and oil refineries of Rangoon burn. (Hulton-Deutsch Collection/Corbis via Getty Images)

8–13 March	1st Battalion, Inniskilling Fusiliers is flown in on board US B-17 bombers to Magwe – the last reinforcements to join Burma Army.
10 March	Burma Army headquarters reopens at Maymyo, near Mandalay.
11 March	US General Joseph Stilwell arrives in Burma and takes titular command of the Chinese Expeditionary Force.
19 March	The I Burma Corps (Burcorps) is formed at Prome, under the command of Lieutenant-General William Slim, where it assumes command of 17th Indian Division, 1st Burma Division and 7th Armoured Brigade.
20–21 March	Japanese air raids destroy Burma Wing (Burwing) on the ground at Magwe.
	Japanese 55th Division advances northwards up the Sittang Valley to Toungoo.
25 March	The Japanese 56th Division lands at Rangoon, and is later deployed in the Sittang Valley.
29–30 March	The Battle of Shwedaung – Burcorps attacks southwards in support of the embattled Chinese and is roundly defeated.
30 March	Toungoo captured from the Chinese 200th Division by Japanese 55th Division and elements of Japanese 56th Division following protracted fighting.
1 April	The Japanese capture Prome.
3 April	Japanese bombers attack Mandalay – engulfing large parts of the wooden city in flames.
7 April	The Japanese 18th Division lands at Rangoon.
11–12 April	The 48th Indian Brigade beats off a Japanese diversionary attack at Kokkogwa.

11 April	The Battle of Yenangyaung begins.
15 April	Lieutenant-General Slim orders the demolition of the Yenangyaung oilfields and oil refinery.
16 April	1st Burma Brigade retreats from the Yin Chaung.
17–19 April	1st Burma Division is encircled by the Japanese 33rd Division at Yenangyaung.
19 April	1st Burma Division breaks out from encirclement at Yenangyaung with the help of the Chinese 38th Division, but abandons most of its wounded, vehicles and heavy equipment.
21 April	Chinese resistance collapses after fierce fighting near Pyinmana opens the way towards Meiktila. The Japanese 56th Division advances into the Shan States.
23 April	General Alexander instructs the bulk of Chinese forces to withdraw to China.
25–26 April	General Alexander orders the withdrawal of the remnants of Burcorps to India and remaining Chinese troops to China.
28 April	1st Burma Division crosses the Irrawaddy River by ferry.
28–29 April	Japanese 18th Division attacks Kyaukse, but is successfully checked by 48th Indian Infantry Brigade.
29 April	General Alexander gives Lieutenant-General Slim the final instruction to withdraw to India.
	Japanese 56th Division captures Lashio – the eastern railhead of the Burma Road – cutting the Burma Road to China.
30 April	Burcorps crosses the Irrawaddy River and the Ava Bridge is demolished at midnight. 1st Burma Division crosses by ferry at Sameikkon.

	The Japanese open fire on Monywa from across the river.
1 May	The Japanese I./215th Regiment captures Monywa on the Chindwin River, beating off fierce counter-attacks by 1st Burma Division.
	Japanese troops of 18th Division occupy Mandalay.
3 May	1st Burma Division and 7th Armoured Brigade withdraw to Ye-u.
4 May	The Governor of Burma, Sir Reginald Dorman-Smith, flies out from Myitkyina to safety in India.
8 May	The Japanese 18th Division captures Myitkyina.
8–9 May	The rearguard of Burcorps reaches Shwegyin, where its main body has been ferried across the Chindwin River to Kalewa. Most of its tanks, guns, vehicles and heavy equipment are destroyed.
9 May	The Japanese attack Shwegyin, but are beaten off until nightfall, when the rearguard withdraws northwards up the riverbank.
11 May	The 48th Indian Infantry Brigade is ferried across the Chindwin River from the eastern bank to Kalewa.
12 May	Burcorps's rearguard leaves Kalewa as the first monsoon rainfall begins.
	The Japanese occupy Kalewa, but do not pursue Burcorps.
19–20 May	The rearguard of Burcorps arrives at Imphal in Manipur State, India and the following day hands over to IV Corps.
20 May	Burma Army is dissolved.

ALLIED COMMANDERS AND FORCES

BRITISH, INDIAN AND BURMESE

The British command structure in Burma before and during the Japanese invasion of Burma was confused and disjointed, undermining successive senior officers' ability to exercise effective command and control, with overall responsibility for Burmese defence being passed from pillar to post. Sackings, battle casualties and tropical disease meant frequent changes in command appointments at all levels were also made during the fighting.

The War Office in London had been made directly responsible for Burmese defence following the political separation of Burma from India in April 1937, it had been GHQ India's responsibility before, with normally a senior Indian Army officer made GOC of the newly formed Burma Army – a tiny administrative headquarters – answerable to the Governor of Burma. In October 1940, the operational defence of Burma was placed under General Headquarters Far East at Singapore, commanded by Air Chief Marshal Sir Robert Brooke-Popham, despite protests from New Delhi. For supply and reinforcements Burma still looked westwards to the War Office and India Command. This meant the GOC Burma Army now reported directly to GHQ Malaya on military matters, the War Office in London for administrative issues and the Governor of Burma for civil affairs. Almost immediately after the Japanese invaded Malaya on 8 December 1941, overall command of Burma was handed back to India Command.

The Commander-in-Chief in India – 59-year-old General Sir Archibald Wavell – was an officer of long and distinguished service, who had been commissioned into the Black Watch in May 1901 and then fought during the Second Boer War and on the North-West Frontier of India in 1908. In January 1909, he attended Staff College, after which Wavell held a series of staff appointments before and during World War I. While acting as a

Field Marshal Sir Archibald Percival Wavell (right) was one of the most gifted senior British commanders of World War II, but during the Retreat from Burma displayed little grasp of the fighting prowess of the Imperial Japanese Army and the comparative weakness of British Commonwealth troops under his command. (Keystone/Getty Images)

The Japanese advance and Allied retreat, January–May 1942

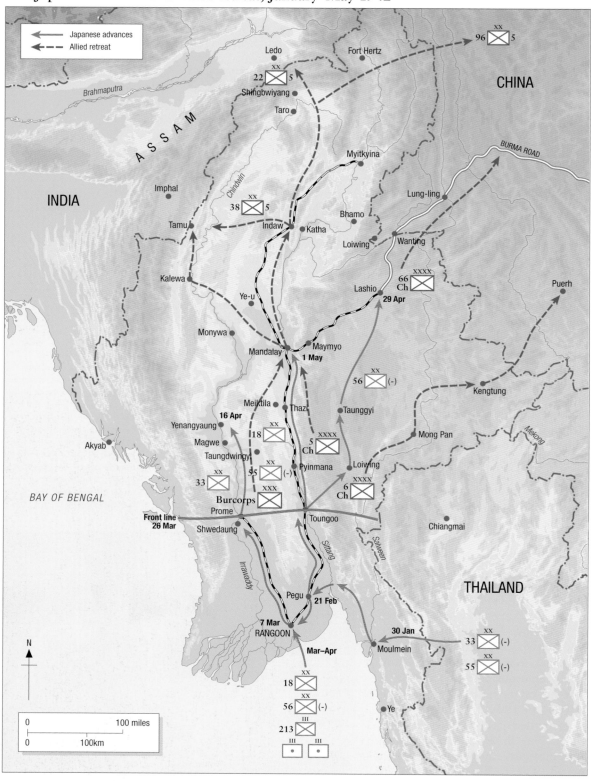

brigade major in France, he lost his left eye. He was awarded a Military Cross for bravery, before holding further senior staff appointments in France, the Caucasus, Egypt and Palestine, ending the war as a temporary brigadier-general. During the inter-war period, Wavell held brigade and divisional command, before being promoted lieutenant-general and appointed GOC British Forces Palestine and Trans-Jordan. Following a brief stint as GOC Southern Command in the UK, Wavell was made GOC-in-Chief of Middle East Command (later redesignated Commander-in-Chief Middle East) with the rank of general. Following the outbreak of World War II, Wavell distinguished himself leading British Commonwealth forces in East Africa and the Middle East against the Italians and Germans, until he was 'kicked upstairs' in July 1941 following British defeats in Greece, Crete and North Africa. A physically and mentally tough, resourceful and largely imperturbable soldier in the face of adversity, Wavell was probably one of the finest British strategic commanders of World War II, as well as being a scholar, philosopher and poet of repute. Despite his age, short stature and the loss of an eye, Wavell cut an imposing figure to his subordinates, although he could be quiet and taciturn, unyielding to opinions at odds with his own deeply held views and was an uninspiring public speaker. Unfortunately, Wavell knew little about Burma, and badly underestimated the Japanese and the weaknesses of his own forces – resulting in repeated orders to hold firm and counter-attack the Japanese whenever possible. On 29 December 1941, Wavell was appointed commander of all Allied troops in a huge area lying between South-East Asia and Australia – ABDACOM (a newly formed joint American, British, Dutch and Australian Command), with his new headquarters in Java. With his theatre-wide responsibilities Wavell only made fleeting trips to Burma until ABDACOM was dissolved on 25 February 1942 and he reverted to only being Commander-in-Chief in India following the fall of Malaya and the Netherlands East Indies.

Lieutenant-General Thomas 'Tom' Hutton was given a poisoned chalice when appointed GOC Burma Army shortly before the Japanese invasion of the colony. (Public domain)

The leadership of Burma Army immediately changed following the Japanese invasion of Malaya, with its commander – Major-General Donald McLeod (an Indian cavalryman nearing retirement) – summarily sacked by Wavell, already alarmed by the lack of preparedness for war in Burma after having visited in October 1941. On 27 December, he was replaced by the Chief of the General Staff in India, Lieutenant-General Thomas 'Tom' Hutton. The new GOC Burma Army was a highly capable staff officer, a glutton for hard work and a man who possessed an acute and well-trained mind, but significantly had never commanded troops in battle. A strong administrative staff accompanied him to Rangoon, with Hutton anticipating months ahead of preparing Burma Army for war before the Japanese invaded. The unprepossessing new GOC and his overburdened and inadequately staffed headquarters immediately faced a wide range of onerous responsibilities, being simultaneously:

General the Hon. Sir Harold Alexander (right), the GOC Burma Army from mid-March 1942, stands in conversation with Sir Reginald Dorman-Smith (left), the Governor of Burma. (Public domain)

an operational headquarters directing the fighting in Tenasserim; a war office dealing with administrative matters; a general headquarters dealing with political affairs (the Chinese); and a line of communications headquarters, that answered to ABDACOM Headquarters, India Command, the Governor and Burmese government, Burma's War Department and the other services. To compound his difficulties Intelligence resources at HQ Burma Army at Rangoon were practically nil. The unexpected collapse of British resistance in Malaya, followed by the pell-mell retreat to Singapore Island, catapulted Burma into the front line under direct threat from Japanese invasion from Thailand. Like his predecessor, the unfortunate Hutton rapidly concluded that Rangoon was the key to the defence of Burma with the two understrength divisions at his disposal, and that it was essential to buy time until reinforcements arrived, since the port provided the only means of landing troops in the country and of keeping the Burma Road open. To prevent its capture he concentrated his meagre forces to block the two entry routes from Thailand: in the southern Shan States and the area between Moulmein and the Sittang River. Burma Army also needed to protect the road running from Rangoon to Moulmein and the forward airbases in Tenasserim. Unfortunately, the overwhelmed Hutton never enjoyed the luxury of time and complete freedom of action from Wavell, who increasingly countermanded his decisions and unfairly questioned his so-called 'defeatist attitude' as the situation quickly deteriorated. To compound his problems, Hutton also had to deal with an ambitious and self-confident divisional commander, who profoundly disagreed with his strategy for defending Burma. The Sittang Bridge debacle, the 'lack of fighting spirit' showed by British Commonwealth troops and the inability of Burma Army to halt the Japanese onrush towards Rangoon claimed Hutton as a victim. On 22 February 1942, Hutton was publicly and embarrassingly sacked having lost the confidence of his superior. The disgraced Hutton was placed in an impossible position, however, being retained as his replacement's chief of staff, largely in recognition that he had done nothing specifically wrong. Unable to bear this demotion and at odds with his superior's later decisions, Hutton resigned and left for India on 26 April 1942, being replaced by Major-General John Winterton.

The dapper General Sir Harold Alexander, who was appointed on 5 March 1942 GOC Burma Army, was very different from his predecessor, having, Wavell believed, the necessary drive, determination and guts to 'grip' the deteriorating situation in Burma. An aristocrat of Anglo-Irish descent, Alexander was commissioned in September 1911 in the Irish Guards, before serving with distinction on the Western Front during World War I, in which he eventually held battalion and brigade command and was awarded the MC and DSO for bravery. Between the wars, he held various staff appointments and studied at the Staff College and Imperial Defence College, before leading a brigade on the North-West Frontier of India in 1934–35. The newly promoted Major-General Alexander was given command of 1st Division in 1938, which he led in France in 1940 before commanding I Corps at Dunkirk. A gifted politician, Alexander, freed from commanding operations on the battlefield, proved well suited to his new role at GHQ Burma Army, where he concentrated on dealing with the Chinese, maintaining a force in being to defend central Burma and extricating the Burma Army from encirclement.

The small, close-knit and highly professional Indian Army provided the highly experienced British officers who led 1st Burma Division and the improvised 17th Indian Division.

The command of 1st Burma Division was held by newly promoted Acting Major-General James Bruce Scott, with initially 13th Indian Infantry Brigade and the newly organized 1st Burma Infantry Brigade (Brigadier G.A. Farwell) and 2nd Burma Infantry Brigade (Brigadier A.J. Bourke) under its command when it formed in July 1941 at Toungoo. This embryonic formation was critically short of artillery, engineers, signals, transport and other units; however, Bruce Scott was required to make it an effective fighting division. The 48-year-old Bruce Scott had been commissioned in the Indian Army in

A group photograph of senior British commanders in Burma in March 1942. From left to right: Major-General James Bruce Scott, Sir John Wise (political adviser to the Governor), General the Hon. Sir Harold Alexander, General Sir Archibald Wavell, Lieutenant-General William Slim and Brigadier H.L. 'Taffy' Davies. (Public domain)

Major-General John 'Jackie' Smyth VC led 17th Indian Division during the initial phase of the Japanese invasion of southern Burma. Following the fighting at the Sittang Bridge, he was summarily sacked, and made a scapegoat for the disaster. (Public domain)

1912, and served with several Indian regiments during World War I, seeing service in France, Egypt, Aden and later East Africa, where he was wounded and awarded a Military Cross for bravery. During the inter-war period, he served as a regimental officer on the North-West Frontier interspersed with holding a succession of staff appointments, before being made commanding officer (CO) of the I./8th Gurkha Rifles in November 1936. Bruce Scott had considerable experience of Burma, having been commander of the Maymyo Brigade in northern Burma since June 1939.

The 17th Indian Division, a motorized formation intended for deployment in Iraq that was broken up piecemeal to serve in Malaya and Burma, was commanded by Major-General John Smyth ('Jackie' to his family and close friends) – an ambitious, brave, resourceful and highly experienced front-line commander, who had been commissioned into the 15th Ludhiana Sikhs in 1912 and had been awarded a Victoria Cross in France during World War I. A highly capable regimental and staff officer, who attended the Staff College in the UK in 1922–23 and then became an instructor at Camberley, the self-confident Smyth had years of experience behind him on the North-West Frontier (earning a Military Cross for bravery in Waziristan in 1920), and then commanded a brigade in the British Expeditionary Force in 1940 in France. A man of strong views and at times a difficult subordinate, Smyth was strongly opposed to deploying his poorly trained division widely dispersed over southern Burma, preferring instead to fight concentrated at a time and place of his own choosing. Although 'visibly composed, cheerful and radiating confidence', unknown to his superiors, Smyth was a seriously sick man suffering from an extremely painful and debilitating anal fissure. The Sittang Disaster put paid to Smyth's career on 1 March (when he was sacked in a search for a scapegoat), with his chief of staff (Cowan) taking over command of 17th Indian Division for the rest of the Burma campaign. Major-General David Tennant 'Punch' Cowan (nicknamed after the traditionally ugly puppet in seaside Punch and Judy shows), a veteran of World War I who had been awarded the Military Cross, had been commissioned into the Indian Army in March 1918 and briefly served with the war-raised IV./3rd Gurkha Rifles. Following World War I, Cowan alternated between regimental service with the I./6th Gurkha Rifles on the North-West Frontier and various staff appointments, finally becoming the CO of the regiment in 1939. Following the outbreak of war, Cowan held various staff appointments at GHQ India, including Director of Military Training, before being sent to Burma.

The arrival of a long-overdue and frequently requested corps headquarters from India Command on 19 March 1942, following the fall of Rangoon, to conduct day-to day operations rectified a major flaw in the British command structure. It freed Lieutenant-General Alexander and Burma Army headquarters at Maymyo at long last to give higher direction to the campaign and handle complex administrative and political problems at its new location, especially managing relations with the Nationalist Chinese.

The I Burma Corps, or simply 'Burcorps', took over operational command of the fighting on 13 March 1942, with 17th Indian Division, 1st Burma Division and 7th Armoured Brigade under command. Its newly appointed corps commander Lieutenant-General William Slim had enjoyed a long and successful career, having initially served as a 2nd lieutenant in the Royal Warwickshire Regiment at Gallipoli and in Mesopotamia, where he was promoted captain and awarded a Military Cross. Following World War I, Slim joined the Indian Army, serving with the I./6th Gurkha Rifles, and rose steadily through the ranks. A 'thinking soldier', Slim passed out top of the Staff College at Quetta, after which he served as a General Staff Office Grade II (GSOII) at GHQ New Delhi and then held the coveted post of Indian Army instructor at the Staff College at Camberley in the UK. After attending the Imperial Defence College in 1938, Slim was promoted lieutenant-colonel and given command of the II./7th Gurkha Rifles. Following the outbreak of war in September 1939, Slim proved himself again in the field as commander of 10th Indian Infantry Brigade in Italian East Africa, where he was wounded. Following a brief stint as a staff officer while recovering, he was appointed GOC 10th Indian Division, which he commanded in action in Iraq and Syria. Slim was cool, calm and imperturbable – traits that proved vital between March and May 1942 – and a soldier's general, with 'Uncle Bill' quickly striking up a close rapport with his exhausted British, Indian and Gurkha troops. Burcorps was a corps headquarters in name only, however, being sadly deficient in radios, signallers, transport and office equipment. Senior staff officers were 'pillaged' from Burma Army or hurriedly flown in from India to fill gaps. The CO and tiny staff of Burcorps quickly gelled, with most officers – Taffy Davies (Brigadier, General Staff), F.C. Simpson, Brian Montgomery (GSOII), Walter Walker (GSOIII) and Godfrey Welchman (Commander, Royal Artillery) – knowing each other well – with Slim quickly earning the unstinting support and loyalty of his subordinates. Slim knew his divisional commanders very well – both James Bruce Scott and 'Punch' Cowan were old friends of 20 years' standing and had served together in the 6th Gurkha Rifles.

The senior British officers selected for higher and divisional command in Burma were given formations and units far from fit to fight against a first-class opponent, being badly below the strength, scales of equipment

A post-war photograph of Lieutenant-General William Slim, who was given command of Burcorps on 19 March 1942. This charismatic officer proved one of the most able British commanders during the retreat from Burma and went on to lead Fourteenth Army between 1943 and 1945. (Bettman via Getty Images)

and above all training needed to defend the colony against a Japanese attack. The competing demands of different theatres of war in 1941 meant the Far East came last behind the immediate needs of defending the UK, holding the Middle East and supplying the USSR with war materiel. Malaya Command still commanded the lion's share of available reinforcements as the primary shield of Britain's colonial possessions in the Far East, with Burma Army remaining critically short of men and materiel sufficient to mount a credible defence, despite the growing 'threat' from Japan. The tempo of military life in the colony gradually increased, with some hesitant steps undertaken between 1940 and 1941 to place the garrison on a war footing, despite an acute shortage of money, including the addition of two companies of sappers and miners. An additional four battalions of the Burma Rifles were raised, doubling the regiment's strength, by stripping officers and NCOs from British units and enlisting Burmese and domiciled Indians (in 1939, the Burma Defence Force contained only 472 Burmese and 3,197 Karens, Chins and Kachins). The strength of the Burma Frontier Force also grew, with units in Tenasserim and the Shan States being placed under military command, organized into small mobile columns or detachments (some mounted on horseback) and tasked with guarding airfields, garrisoning key points, protecting the flanks of regular units and harassing invading troops. Unfortunately, the short-term cost of this rapid expansion of the Burmese garrison was of lowering their military effectiveness, with shortages of arms, ammunition and equipment badly hampering training. Stocks of weapons, ammunition, vehicles and sundry medical and other defence stores remained non-existent, particularly artillery, anti-aircraft and anti-tank weapons.

The Burmese garrison was heavily augmented by forces drawn from India Command in 1941, reflecting increasing concerns about the threat posed by imperial Japan. The 13th Indian Infantry Brigade, commanded by Brigadier Arthur Curtis, landed at Rangoon between March and April 1941, and was followed by 16th Indian Infantry Brigade, led by Brigadier J.K. 'Jonah'

A British officer instructs a group of young recruits serving in the Burma Rifles in how to use a Bren light machine gun. Few had received adequate training before the Japanese invasion began. (Pictorial Press Ltd/Alamy)

Jones, at the end of November 1941. Further reinforcements from India were en route or quickly despatched following the Japanese invasion of Malaya, including the headquarters of 17th Indian Division and 46th Indian Infantry Brigade, and a little later 48th Indian Infantry Brigade. The Indian formations sent to Burma contained units that bore the proud titles of regiments with long and distinguished service to the King-Emperor, but were dissimilar in nearly all other respects. Most were a pale shadow of the experienced and highly professional prewar regular army, being products of the massive expansion of the Indian Army since the outbreak of World War II to meet imperial needs in the Middle East, Malaya and Hong Kong. This had been achieved by the repeated 'milking' of regular army units and then successive waves of 'new' units of experienced officers, NCOs and men, who, along with young, raw and inexperienced recruits with barely three months' service and badly lacking in basic training, formed 'hostilities only' units. This process had been repeated on several occasions, with a corresponding short-term fall in the overall combat effectiveness of the entire Indian Army. The extremely weak units sent to Burma, moreover, were organized, equipped and trained for desert warfare in the Middle East, where the Indian Army was heavily committed, with most units accompanied by tracked and wheeled first-line transport unsuited to fighting off-road in the jungles of southern Burma. None had been given adequate specialized training to live, move and fight in the jungle against a Japanese opponent, whose fighting ability was badly underestimated by British commanders at all levels.

A disgruntled-looking British soldier of the pre-war British garrison stands guard over a pile of bedding rolls. Two British battalions normally formed part of the Burma Army during peacetime. (Photo by Wolfgang Weber/ullstein bild via Getty Images)

The British, Indian and Burmese troops who fought in Burma were armed and equipped on common British Commonwealth lines and shared the same basic doctrine. The .303 Lee-Enfield – a bolt-action rifle with a ten-round magazine – was the standard infantry weapon used by British Commonwealth fighting troops, with each infantry section also equipped with a .303 Bren light machine gun. This highly effective and extremely reliable automatic weapon had a two-man crew and was fed by a 30-round magazine. The tripod-mounted .303 Vickers medium machine gun and 3in. mortar provided heavier fire support within each infantry battalion. Officers carried the Webley pistol as a sidearm.

The army in Burma had very weak artillery support at the beginning of the campaign, having just four mountain batteries, equipped with tried and tested 3.7in. howitzers, with a range of 6,000 yards, that could be broken down into pieces and carried by mules. The 1st Indian Field Artillery Regiment – one of the last reinforcements to land at Rangoon – brought with it 16 25pdr guns, capable of lobbing a high-explosive shell 13,400 yards. A single battery of 25pdr guns formed part of 7th Armoured Brigade, in addition to an anti-tank battery equipped with 2pdr anti-tank guns.

Burma Army had only a handful of antiquated Rolls-Royce armoured cars at its disposal in 1941, equipped with Vickers machine guns, manned by men of the Burma Auxiliary Force. The deployment of 7th Armoured Brigade brought with it two highly experienced, battle-hardened regiments, each equipped with 55 Stuart light tanks. These mechanically reliable tracked armoured fighting vehicles, capable of a speed of 36mph, were armed with a 37mm main gun and two machine guns. Unfortunately, the main armament could only fire solid armour-piercing shot, limiting its effectiveness on the battlefield.

The strength of the RAF allocated to defend Burma before the war was tiny. No. 60 Squadron, equipped with Blenheim light bombers, was deployed in February 1941 (it later moved to Malaya and never returned), and then in September 1941, No. 67 Squadron was deployed, equipped with 18 Brewster Buffalo fighters. US volunteers of the American Volunteer Group (AVG), equipped with P-40B Tomahawks, landed in Burma during the summer of 1941, ostensibly to train for protecting the Burma Road, with one squadron allocated to the defence of Rangoon. Under the command of Air Vice Marshal Donald Stevenson from 1 January 1942, this tiny force – No. 221 Group, RAF Burma – gradually increased, and by early March consisted of two squadrons of Hawker Hurricanes, two of Blenheim light bombers and two of Lysander army cooperation aircraft. A combination of steady attrition and heavy bombing raids on Magwe on 20/21 March 1942 led to the complete evacuation of Burma by the RAF, leaving Burcorps bereft of air support.

Brewster Buffalo fighters flying in formation in the Far East in late 1941. Around 150 Buffalos comprised the bulk of the British fighter defences of Burma, Malaya and Singapore just prior to the Japanese invasions, divided among two RAAF, two RAF and one RNZAF squadrons. In the air, the Buffalo performed poorly against the Mitsubishi A6M Zero, with only a handful surviving. (D and S Photography Archives/Alamy)

CHINESE

The British high command initially rejected Generalissimo Chiang Kai-Shek's offers in December 1941 of Nationalist troops to defend Burma, apart from a single division – mindful of long-term Chinese territorial claims on the colony, the political need for Burma to be defended by British troops and lastly the acute logistical difficulties that supplying them entailed. The deployment of the Chinese Expeditionary Force following the fall of Rangoon to repel the Japanese advance towards Mandalay proved vital, but complicated overall command in Burma, with misunderstanding and mutual distrust between Chiang Kai-Shek and Alexander over each other's long-term political intentions in the colony bedevilling relations. A casualty of this mutual distrust was a lack of effective cooperation between the British and Chinese at all levels of command, just when close coordination and mutual support was badly required.

The titular overall command of all Chinese forces in Burma was given by Generalissimo Chiang Kai-Shek to 58-year-old Lieutenant-General Joseph Stilwell, a senior US army officer, who arrived on 4 March 1942 in China. Stilwell's other varied duties included being the military representative of the US President to China, Generalissimo Chiang Kai-Shek's chief of staff in his capacity as Allied Supreme Commander in the China Theatre, commander of all US forces in the American-designated China–Burma–India (CBI) region, controller of Lend Lease supplies sent to China and administrator of the Burma Road. This announcement caused the British high command great consternation, as it broke an earlier agreement that all Chinese forces in Burma would come under General Alexander's command. A solution was eventually found when the abrasive Stilwell (his difficult manner had long before earnt him his nickname 'Vinegar Joe') willingly placed himself on 24 March under General Alexander's 'general direction', to coordinate operations with

Colonel Liu Fangwu commanded the Chinese 113th Regiment during the Battle of Yenangyaung. (Public domain)

Burcorps. The command structure of the Chinese Expeditionary Force (CEF) in reality proved far, far more complicated, as Stilwell discovered himself when setting up headquarters at Maymyo. When he visited Alexander, Stilwell discovered General Tu Tu-Ming, the commander of Chinese Fifth Army, had already introduced himself as the commander of the CEF (he was himself eventually replaced by General Luo Zhuoying). The defence of Toungoo quickly exposed the limitations of Stilwell's authority when General Tu Tu-Ming ignored his orders to send the Chinese 22nd Division to support the beleaguered Chinese 200th Division. Indeed, the unfortunate Stilwell quickly realized he had command in name only, lacking powers to give orders or enforce them, with senior Chinese officers at army, divisional and even regimental level avoiding taking action that might cause losses to their 'personal armies' or at odds with what they thought the Generalissimo wanted, without referring the American's orders up the chain of command for his approval. Following a direct confrontation with the Generalissimo at Chunking, on 6 April Chiang and his wife travelled to Maymyo to inform assembled Chinese commanders of Stilwell's authority over them; but at the same time, an official seal given to authenticate his instructions named him as Chief Advisor/Chief of Staff and not Commander-in-Chief of the CEF. Despite these changes, orders issued by General Alexander and Stilwell still needed the agreement of the Chinese General Staff Mission at Burma Army's HQ, headed by General Lin-Wei, and ultimately the cautious Chiang Kai-Shek. To further complicate matters, General Lin-Wei frequently issued his own often-conflicting orders as the military situation deteriorated and effectively collapsed early in May 1942, when Stilwell and Luo Zhuoying retreated to India, leaving their subordinates to decide their own fate.

The leadership of senior Chinese officers at army and divisional level proved very mixed. None had experience of fighting alongside allies, and effective cooperation between the British and Chinese officers at all levels was further handicapped by lack of interpreters, liaison officers and maps.

The CEF, which gradually deployed in Burma between January and April 1942 and fielded somewhere between 70,000 and 130,000 men, was made up of some of the best fighting troops Nationalist China had available: Fifth Army (200th, 22nd and 96th divisions, with attached tank and artillery units) under the leadership of General Tu Tu-Ming; Sixth Army (the 49th, 93rd and Temporary 55th divisions) led by General Kan Li-Chu; and Sixty-Sixth Army (New 28th, New 29th and New 38th divisions) under General Chang Chen's command. This order of battle looked very impressive on paper, but the combat effectiveness of the Chinese Nationalist divisions that fought in Burma varied enormously, being a 'hodgepodge' and 'a mixture of elite, ordinary and inefficient formations' according to one Chinese historian – although their ranks were filled with tough, hardy and self-reliant soldiers (many with recent combat experience of fighting the Japanese). The combat performance

A young Indian sepoy explains how a .303 Lee-Enfield rifle works to a pair of serious-looking Chinese soldiers. (Northcliffe Collection/ANL/Shutterstock)

The generally well-equipped Chinese Nationalist troops deployed in Burma employed a wide variety of weapons and equipment. These infantrymen are wearing M35 steel helmets bought in bulk from Nazi Germany. (Trinity Mirror/Mirrorpix/Alamy)

of Chinese armies and divisions depended in large part on their commanders, with some proving highly skilled and others appallingly bad at their profession. The English-speaking General Sun Li-Jen, GOC 38th Division, was considered one of the best, being characterized as 'intelligent, energetic and alert' by his British counterparts, but having 'little sense of time' when it came to coordinating operations. Similarly, General Peng Pi-Shen, commanding 49th Division, was considered an able and forceful commander, but one who repeatedly refused to take offensive action without permission from his superiors. Other Chinese divisional commanders proved indecisive, incompetent and generally unfit for command. Stilwell's staff characterized General Kan Li-Chu, for example, as lacking both ability and imagination, and if faced with an adverse situation, likely to break down.

The battle-hardened Chinese 200th Division – 8,500 strong – was by far the best Chinese Nationalist division, having light tanks, motor vehicles and US Lend Lease 75mm howitzers and 105mm guns. Similarly, the New 38th Division, whose officers and men were highly trained on Western lines, was well equipped with European and US weapons and had considerable combat experience fighting both communists and the Japanese. Most Chinese divisions were much weaker – fielding approximately 6,000 men – and made up of poorly trained and ill-equipped infantry, and were badly short of anti-tank guns, field artillery and other heavy weapons. A few, like the Temporary 56th Division, were newly organized, and their unfortunate, largely untrained conscripts were only issued rifles after the campaign began. Many Chinese formations lacked transportation and marched into battle on foot, with unarmed coolies carrying weapons, equipment and supplies, although vehicles were later provided by 'borrowing' US lorries from the Burma Road. An organized supply and administrative system was marked by its absence, and when British resources failed to provide food and petrol, the Chinese lived like 'locusts off the land', stealing freely from the unfortunate Burmese population. Sadly, medical units were also virtually non-existent, with the Chinese relying on British resources and a medical unit run by Dr Gordon Seagrave, an American missionary, for the care of the sick and wounded.

A large memorial and wall relief in the grounds of the Hote Wan Temple in Toungoo commemorates the Chinese Expeditionary Force in Burma, and in particular the dogged defence of the town by the 200th Division in March 1942. (Xinhua/Alamy)

JAPANESE COMMANDERS AND FORCES

The Japanese high command in Tokyo viewed conquering Burma as an integral part of its wider strategy in South-East Asia in 1941–42, with the British colony forming an outer defensive bulwark for its other newly conquered territories in the Far East: Malaya, Singapore, Borneo and in particular the vital oilfields of the Netherland East Indies, upon which it depended for fuel, that would effectively be placed out of range of Allied aircraft by its capture. It would also sever the US supply line to Chinese Nationalist forces doggedly defying imperial Japanese forces in south-west China by cutting off badly needed US Lend Lease supplies sustaining its war effort. Lastly, the rice grown by the 'rice basket' of South-East Asia and the timber, oil and scarce wolfram produced in Burma, moreover, was viewed of vital economic importance to sustaining the long-term Japanese war effort and so-called Greater East Asia Co-Prosperity Sphere.

The Japanese command structure for the invasion of Burma was straightforward when compared to that of their British Commonwealth opponents and remained largely unchanged for the duration of the campaign. As part of the Southern Expeditionary Army Group, under the overall command of Field Marshal Count Terauchi at Saigon, the 35,000-strong Fifteenth Army was tasked with occupying Thailand and then invading Burma, with Rangoon being the immediate objective, if its sister Twenty-Fifth Army made rapid progress down the Malayan Peninsula towards Singapore. The 54-year-old Lieutenant-General Shojiro Iida, commanding Fifteenth Army, was a well-experienced, highly intelligent and well-educated professional soldier, born into a military family from Yamaguchi Prefecture in Japan. He had enjoyed a successful career, including leading the 4th Imperial Guards

Field Marshal Count Terauchi was appointed overall commander of the Japanese Southern Expeditionary Army Group in November 1941, responsible for the conquest of South-East Asia and the South-West Pacific. (Photo by Heinrich Hoffmann/ullstein bild via Getty Images)

Regiment, before holding a succession of senior staff appointments in China and Japan. In August 1939, he commanded the Japanese Army garrison on Formosa (Taiwan) and then briefly Twenty-Fifth Army in Indo-China.

Fifteenth Army was allocated two infantry divisions: 55th Division, and the highly regarded 33rd Division, both of which were understrength – fielding two infantry regiments instead of the normal three. They were accompanied by only a small quantity of mountain artillery and other supporting arms. Both relied on pack animals (mules, horses and oxen) for transport and supply, given the routes from Thailand into Burma were little more than rough mountain tracks running through dense jungle.

The 55th Division was led by Lieutenant-General Hiroshi Takeuchi, who had commanded 49th Infantry Regiment in 1936–37, and then held various staff appointments before being given divisional command in April 1941. The division's cadre was brought up to full strength with reservists and conscripts in October 1941; it lacked combat experience as a formation, but had been given some training in the jungles on Formosa. It proved slow and 'sticky' during the invasion of Burma, however, which reflected poorly upon its commander. It was probably due to his lack of drive and determination (in turn displayed by his formation) that he was retired from the army in 1943. In stark contrast, the well-regarded commander of the 33rd Division – 52-year-old Lieutenant-General Seizo Sakurai – was already well known for his drive, determination and aggressiveness, having performed extremely well in China as a regimental and staff officer. In December 1940, Sakurai was promoted lieutenant-general, and the following year was given command of 33rd Division, then serving as part of the Eleventh Army in China.

Other formations were 'on call' for the invasion of Burma, including 56th Division held back in Japan due to lack of shipping, and others freed for redeployment if the invasion of Malaya proceeded well. The newly formed 56th Division was led by Lieutenant-General Masao Watanabe, who had held a succession of staff appointments, served as head of the Army Armaments Factory and then instructed at various training establishments before being given command in August 1940. Despite having comparatively little combat experience, Watanabe proved highly successful at directing fast-moving motorized operations in northern Burma. The 18th Division, commanded by Lieutenant-General Renya Mutuguchi, was chosen to reinforce the troops in Burma following the surrender of Malaya Command on 15 February 1942 and brief service in the Phillipines. A member of the rising military clique – Mutuguchi and his 1st Infantry Regiment had been involved in the Marco Polo Bridge Incident between 7 and 11 July 1937 that had triggered the Second Sino-Japanese War – he had served as Commandant of the Military School in April 1940 before being appointed commander of 18th Division, which had only played a limited role in the Malayan campaign.

The Japanese Army air forces allocated to support Fifteenth Army, under the overall leadership of General Sakaguchi at Southern Area headquarters, consisted of the highly experienced, well-trained and well-equipped 5th Air Division commanded by Lieutenant-General Hideyoshi Obata. It consisted of a mixture of mostly modern fighters, bombers and other more specialized aircraft, including Ki-27 Nate and Ki-43-II Oscar fighters, and Ki-46 Dinah and Ki-21 Sally bombers. Further support came from 3rd Air Division when required for a major operation. The aviators of 5th Air Division initially

Colonel Aung San was one of the key Burmese leaders of the Burma Independence Army. He is pictured with his wife Daw Khin Kyi in 1942. (Public domain)

met stern resistance, suffering heavy losses from the RAF and AVG. The destruction of Burwing at Magwe gave Japanese airmen virtually complete command of the air for the last stage of the campaign, granting them freedom to carry out tactical air support and range over Burma bombing at will.

The Japanese Fifteenth Army was accompanied by the initially 300-strong Burma Independence Army (BIA) that had formed at Bangkok on 30 December 1941. It consisted of fervent Burmese nationalists, drawn from the Thakin movement, led by Aung San and its Japanese supporters under Colonel Suzuki Keiji of the former Minami Kikan intelligence organization, who believed Imperial Japan offered Burma the best means of securing its independence from Britain. This small band of patriots provided Fifteenth Army with guides and interpreters, gathered vital intelligence, spread

A cheering crowd greet a group of young Burmese volunteers serving with the Burma Independence Army outside Rangoon. (Public domain)

propaganda and collected food for advancing Japanese troops, who were warmly welcomed by the Burmese population. As the Japanese advanced, the BIA's strength swelled, and by the time Rangoon fell it fielded 10,000–12,000 men, primarily equipped with captured British small arms and equipment. Enthusiasm proved no substitute for training, and on several occasions BIA troops suffered badly on the battlefield at British hands.

The Imperial Japanese Army was primarily a force of highly trained light infantry, with many of its officers, NCOs and men having seen recent combat experience in China. A combination of light infantry skills, very light scales of personal equipment and living off the land enabled frugal Japanese to manoeuvre freely off-road in difficult jungle-covered terrain, using the cover and concealment it provided to infiltrate through or go around enemy positions and encircle them. Few had received specialist instruction in living, moving and fighting in the jungle, which many Japanese troops also initially found a terrifying and confusing environment. Most Japanese infantryman carried a bolt action Type 99 Arisaka Rifle, which fired a 7.7mm round and had an effective range of 3,400m, and could be fitted with a Type 30 bayonet for close-quarters fighting. Several Type 97 fragmentation hand grenades, triggered by banging the striker on a hard surface before being thrown, added to an infantryman's load. No sub-machine guns were employed in 1942. Each infantry section normally had a rugged and generally reliable air-cooled Type 96 light machine gun (LMG); it had a bipod and a crew of two men, and fired 6.5mm rounds from a 30-round curved box magazine. Unlike other LMGs of its type, it could be fitted with a bayonet. The heavier tripod-mounted Type 92 heavy machine gun – firing 30-round strips of 7.7mm ammunition at a rate of 400–500 rounds per minute – proved a highly effective source of sustained fire support for Japanese troops in attack and defence, equipping a machine-gun company in each infantry battalion. Each gun had a three-man crew and had a range of up to 4,900 yards although its effective range was 875 yards. Officers normally carried a Type 14 Nambu semi-automatic pistol (with an eight-round magazine) or similar as a sidearm, and a sword in the field for personal protection.

By European standards Japanese artillery was extremely weak. The Japanese relied on mountain guns for direct and indirect artillery support, with each division having one mountain artillery regiment equipped with 75mm Type 94 mountain guns, capable of being broken down into parts and man-packed or carried by pack animals along tracks otherwise impassable to wheeled vehicles. An infantry gun platoon in each infantry battalion provided close fire support, equipped with two older Type 41 75mm mountain guns with a range of 6,900 yards. Some units were equipped with Type 92 70mm infantry guns – a light howitzer with a range up to 3,050 yards used normally in a direct fire role. To counter British tanks and armoured cars, 33rd Division fielded only four 37mm anti-tank guns, with its infantry relying on Molotov cocktails or improvised explosive charges for protection.

A Japanese infantryman leads the way ahead of an elephant ridden by a mahout during a river crossing. The Japanese Fifteenth Army made use of a wide range of transport animals during the initial stage of the invasion of southern Burma. (Universal History Archive/UIG via Getty images)

The Fifteenth Army enjoyed far greater artillery support after the capture of Rangoon, which resulted in the deployment of several artillery regiments, equipped with 105mm field and 150mm medium artillery.

The 33rd Division had been supported by a single platoon of four Type 95 Ha-Go light tanks (detached from the 2nd Tank Regiment) during the initial invasion. One was lost crossing the Salween River and the other three were destroyed at Pegu by British armour, whose crews were astounded by how badly they were handled in battle. Each very lightly armoured 7.4-ton tank was equipped with a 37mm gun and two 7.7mm light machine guns. Following the fall of Rangoon, the 1st Tank Regiment and 14th Tank Regiment were deployed in Burma, equipped with both Type 95 light tanks and heavier Type 97 Chi-Ha medium tanks, armed with a 57mm gun and two 7.7mm machine guns. The obvious deficiencies of their own weakly armed, mechanically unreliable and lightly armoured AFVs perhaps accounts for the speed with which the Japanese pressed captured Stuart light tanks into service during the later stages of the campaign.

ORDERS OF BATTLE

BURMA ARMY OUTLINE ORDER OF BATTLE, 20 JANUARY 1942

ARMY HQ (LIEUTENANT-GENERAL T.J. HUTTON), RANGOON

1st Burma Division ('Burdiv') (Major-General J. Bruce Scott), Southern Shan States
1st Burma Brigade (Brigadier G.A.L. Farwell)
    2nd King's Own Yorkshire Light Infantry
    1st Burma Rifles
    5th Burma Rifles
13th Indian Infantry Brigade (Brigadier A.C. Curtis)
    V./1st Punjab Regiment
    II./7th Rajput Regiment
    I./18th Royal Garwhal Rifles
27th Indian Mountain Regiment
56th Field Company, Madras Sappers and Miners
50th Field Park Company, Madras Sappers and Miners
Malerkotla Field Company, Sappers and Miners

17th Indian Division (Major-General J.G. Smyth), Moulmein/Kyaikto
16th Indian Infantry Brigade (Brigadier J.K. 'Jonah' Jones), Kawkareik
    I./9th Battalion Royal Jat Regiment
    I./7th Gurkha Rifles
    4th Burma Rifles (less elements)
    7th Burma Rifles
    1st Burma Field Company
2nd Burma Brigade (Brigadier A.J.H. Bourke), Moulmein
    IV./12th Frontier Force Regiment
    7th Burma Rifles
    8th Burma Rifles
    3rd Burma Rifles (less elements)
    12th (Poonch) Mountain Battery
    3rd Indian Light Anti-Aircraft Battery (one troop of four 40mm Bofors guns)
46th Indian Infantry Brigade (Brigadier Roger Ekin), Bilin River area
    VII./10th Baluch Regiment
    V./17th Dogra Regiment
    III./7th Gurkha Rifles
48th Indian Infantry Brigade (Brigadier Hugh-Jones), en route to Burma
    I./3rd Gurkha Rifles
    I./4th Gurkha Rifles
    II./5th Royal Gurkha Rifles (Frontier Force)
28th Mountain Regiment (less elements)
2nd Indian Anti-Tank Regiment
24th Field Company, Bombay Sappers and Miners
60th Field Company, Madras Sappers and Miners

JAPANESE FIFTEENTH ARMY OUTLINE ORDER OF BATTLE, DECEMBER 1942

FIFTEENTH ARMY HQ (LIEUTENANT-GENERAL S. IIDA)

33rd Division (Lieutenant-General S. Sakurai)
33rd Infantry Group HQ (Major-General M. Araki)
    214th Regiment (Colonel T. Sakuma)
    215th Regiment (Colonel M. Harada)
33rd Mountain Artillery Regiment
33rd Engineer Regiment
33rd Transport Regiment
Divisional medical unit
Two field hospitals
Veterinary section
Ordnance section
One tank troop (four Type 95s detached from 2nd Tank Regiment)
11th Anti-Tank Company

55th Division (Lieutenant-General Y. Takeuchi)
112th Regiment (Colonel K. Obarazawa/Colonel S. Tanahashi)
143rd Regiment (Colonel M. Uno)
55th Cavalry Regiment (less elements)
55th Artillery Regiment (less elements)
55th Engineer Regiment (less elements)
55th Transport Company
Divisional medical unit
One field hospital
Veterinary section
Ordnance section

Army Troops
Two wire communication companies
Two fixed radio units
One line of communication sector unit
Two independent transport companies (motor transport)
Two independent transport companies (horse transport)
One line of communication hospital

THE CAMPAIGN

OPENING ROUNDS: FROM KAWKAREIK TO THE BILIN RIVER

The initial Japanese advance into Burma took place on 12 December 1941, when minor elements of Fifteenth Army crossed the Thai border into Tenasserim and shortly afterwards occupied the airfield at Victoria Point largely without opposition, cutting the Allied air reinforcement route to Malaya. A lull ensued while the Japanese Twenty-Fifth Army rampaged down the Malayan Peninsula towards Singapore Island and the Fifteenth Army secured its rear in Thailand. On 23 December and 25 December, Rangoon was heavily bombed by the Japanese 5th Air Division, causing widespread damage, heavy civilian casualties and serious alarm amongst the Burmese, Anglo-Indian and Indian population. A mass exodus from the city took place aboard ship to India, or else in long columns of refugees trekking eastwards to Arakan or northwards to Upper Burma to safety. Eighteen RAF Brewster Buffaloes and 21 P-40 Tomahawks of the 3rd AVG Squadron offered effective opposition, shooting down ten bombers and five fighters.

Rangoon citizens run for cover as Japanese bombers approach the Burmese capital in December 1941. (Public domain)

Fifteenth Army advanced in strength from Thailand into Burma at 0500hrs on 20 January, along a rough track running through the Kawkareik Pass in the 6,800ft-high Dawna Range. The 55th Division, accompanied by members of the newly formed Burma Independence Army, advanced in widely separated columns, and quickly made its way through dense jungle towards the large river port of Moulmein. Much further south a single detached battalion – the III./112th Regiment – had already crossed the Tenasserim Range and quickly seized the town of Tavoy on 19 January, destroying the 6th Burma Rifles in the process. The now-isolated garrison of Mergui further south had to be quickly withdrawn, giving the Japanese control of all three airfields in southern Tenasserim.

The main weight of the Japanese offensive fell on 17th Indian Division, commanded by Major-General John Smyth, whose newly arrived headquarters had just taken control of the two widely dispersed brigades blocking its advance: 16th Indian Infantry Brigade and 2nd Burma Brigade. 1st Burma Division (Burdiv) – watching the border in the southern Shan States in north-eastern Burma (shielding Mandalay and the Burma Road), with 1st Burma and 13th Indian Infantry brigades under its command – was initially left unengaged. The first clash of arms of the Japanese invasion took place early on 20 January at Myawadi, 38 miles in advance of the main defensive position covering the Thai border held by the newly deployed 16th Indian Infantry Brigade, commanded by Brigadier 'Jonah' Jones, at the town of Kawkareik. The Japanese made short work of a single isolated company of the I./7th Gurkha Rifles not far from the frontier (D Company later made good its escape from Japanese encirclement) forcing the rest of the battalion – after an attempt to relieve it – to withdraw at dusk to Sukhali. A lorry-borne patrol of the I./9th Royal Jat Regiment proved more successful during a brief encounter battle with the leading elements of the Japanese 55th Reconnaissance Regiment on the Palu–Kwingale track, but during the evening, the battalion lost a complete infantry company at Kwingale south of Myawadi, whose handful of survivors dispersed into the jungle to escape on foot. The main defensive position at Kawkareik was judged untenable by Brigadier Jones fearing encirclement of 16th Indian Infantry Brigade following the loss of Kwingale (which had exposed his right flank); at 1800hrs on 21 January, Jones ordered the destruction of still desert-camouflaged surplus vehicles, stores and equipment and a withdrawal towards Moulmein later that night. The bewildered, raw, ill-equipped and poorly trained fighting troops making up his command – already disorientated and demoralized by fighting in dense jungle – left as planned on foot or aboard vehicles, with the I./9th Royal Jat Regiment acting as rearguard. The initial stage of the withdrawal went horribly wrong, however, when the leading lorry of the brigade's motor transport column, heavily overloaded with ammunition, accidentally sank as it disembarked the only ferry crossing the Kyaing River eight miles from Kawkareik, forcing the hurried destruction of all other remaining second-line wheeled transport. Utter confusion reigned amongst the now badly demoralized British, Indian and Gurkha troops from brigade headquarters downwards as they withdrew in chaos to Kyondo, until a semblance of order was restored the following day. The routed 16th Indian Infantry Brigade – after destroying all of its remaining wheeled vehicles, letting loose mules and throwing heavy weapons into the water – crossed the Gyaing River aboard hurriedly collected small boats, and trudged on foot down the southern riverbank towards safety. On 24 January, the demoralized, badly beaten and exhausted main body was rescued by river steamers and transported eventually to Martaban to rest, recover and re-equip, having lost all its vehicles, heavy weapons and most of its mule transport. Many men arrived infected with malaria.

The initial fighting in the Dawna Hills provided a grim foretaste of things to come, with the victorious Japanese 55th Division having inflicted a bloody defeat on its opponents at little cost to itself. Morale plummeted amongst poorly trained Indian, Gurkha and Burmese troops exposed to the first shock of battle and now deeply fearful of the jungle and 'fanatical' Japanese troops that opposed them. The frugal Japanese infantry had quickly demonstrated their superior ability to live, move and fight in the jungle. They fully exploited the mobility and independence from fixed lines of communication that pack transport and long years of combat experience and light infantry training had given them, to encircle or infiltrate through their opponents to attack command elements and rear-echelon troops or build roadblocks when opportunity offered that cut off forward troops from outside support. In stark contrast, British Commonwealth troops had been tied to the roads by their wheeled first-line and second-line transport, upon which they depended. The threat of or discovery of Japanese troops building roadblocks in their rear, threatening their escape and lines of communication, invariably provoked furious attacks to clear them, and, if they failed, the hurried abandonment of vehicles, equipment and weapons followed by a desperate escape on foot. The fragile morale repeatedly displayed by poorly trained British, Indian and Gurkha troops (a so-called 'lack of will to resist' in official parlance) had been further undermined by characteristic Japanese 'jitter' tactics. Most nights, small parties of Japanese troops or individual soldiers prowled around British positions intermittently shooting, setting off firecrackers and shouting in pigeon-English, causing a serious loss of sleep, repeated bouts of panic and the expenditure of vast amounts of ammunition as the defenders blazed away at often imaginary attackers hiding in the dark, dense and impenetrable jungle.

The defence of the picturesque river port of Moulmein and its 50,000 inhabitants, nestled on the bank of the 1½-mile-wide estuary of the Salween River, was entrusted to 2nd Burma Brigade, initially under the operational command of Brigadier A.H. Bourke and then from noon on 30 January Brigadier Roger Ekin, made up primarily of three Burma Rifle battalions supported by the IV./12th Frontier Force Regiment, 12th (Poonch) Mountain Artillery Battery, four Bofors guns of 3rd Indian Anti-Aircraft Battery and

The bombing of Rangoon and other Burmese cities and towns by Japanese aircraft led to a mass exodus of British, Anglo-Indian and Indian refugees, who sought shelter in the countryside and later India. (© Imperial War Museum, JAR 1230)

The Burma Frontier Force (originally known as the Burma Military Police) was largely made up of men drawn from a range of ethnic groups: Kachins, Karens, Chins and locally domiciled Gurkhas and Indians. (Pictorial Press Ltd/Alamy)

a handful of Indian sappers. A weak detachment of the Burma Frontier Force – 200 strong – guarded the nearby airfield. A sea of dense jungle to the east provided ideal cover for Japanese patrols to close up to the town largely undetected.

The 12-mile-long defensive perimeter proved too much for the available troops, with the already understrength 3rd Burma Rifles quickly giving way at mid-morning on 30 January when Japanese troops attacked in its sector from the east across the Ataran River, before eventually collapsing entirely under heavy mortar fire later that afternoon. The IV./12th Frontier Force Regiment, quickly deployed from reserve onto a commanding north–south ridge within the perimeter that shielded the jetties on the Martaban River, successfully held up the Japanese assault from the east, but further enemy progress was made later that evening against Burma Rifles units to the north and south of Moulmein that threatened both ends of the ridge. The only bright spot was the airfield, where 200 Sikhs held out for 24 hours under heavy attack, before escaping on foot to Martaban. A lengthy defence of Moulmein was now clearly impossible, given the unreliability some Burmese units had displayed during the initial fighting. The garrison was being slowly squeezed backwards into a smaller and smaller perimeter, with the wide river at its back isolating it from external support. A decision to withdraw was made by Major-General Smyth at midnight after Brigadier Roger Ekin advised he doubted the town could be held the following day. Early in the morning of 31 January, 2nd Burma Brigade made good its escape across the Gulf of Martaban aboard 15 river steamers – albeit abandoning its transport,

The Battle of Moulmein, 30–31 January 1942

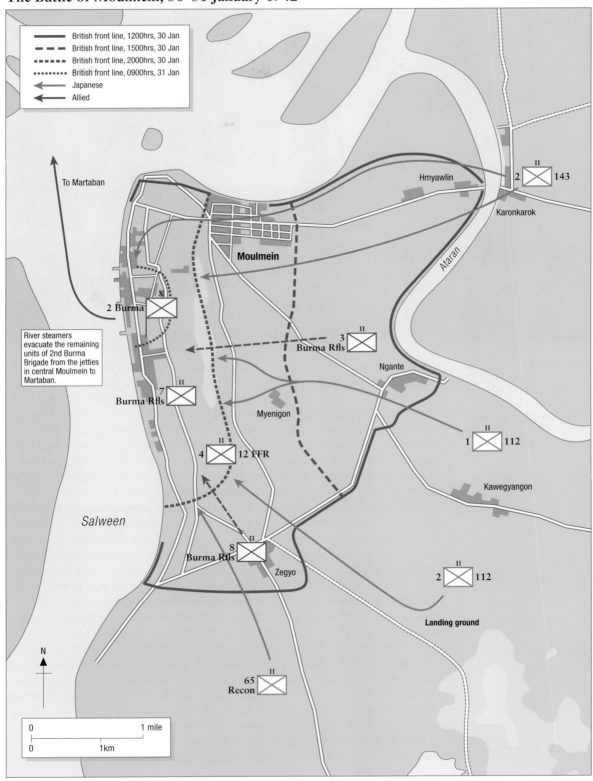

Legend:
- British front line, 1200hrs, 30 Jan
- British front line, 1500hrs, 30 Jan
- British front line, 2000hrs, 30 Jan
- British front line, 0900hrs, 31 Jan
- Japanese
- Allied

To Martaban

Hmyawlin

Karonkarok

2 | 143

Moulmein

Ataran

2 Burma

X

River steamers evacuate the remaining units of 2nd Burma Brigade from the jetties in central Moulmein to Martaban.

3 Burma Rfls

Ngante

7 Burma Rfls

Myenigon

1 | 112

4 | 12 FFR

Kawegyangon

Salween

8 Burma Rfls

Zegyo

2 | 112

Landing ground

N

65 Recon

0   1 mile
0   1km

A column of Japanese infantry, led by officers mounted on horseback, pass a crowd of Burmese onlookers near Martaban during the initial phase of the invasion. (Bettman via Getty Images)

anti-aircraft guns and large quantities of food, ammunition and stores. The IV./12th Frontier Force, 8th Burma Rifles and mountain battery acted as a rearguard during the final evacuation, which ended at 1000hrs when the last vessel left Moulmein. Only a single river steamer was sunk by Japanese shellfire from guns hurriedly deployed on the ridge during the crossing to Martaban. Overall, the rearguard action at Moulmein had been a creditable performance for British arms when compared to the debacle in the Dawna Hills, but worryingly it indicated that the combat effectiveness of many Burmese units making up Burma Army was low.

The speed and ferocity of Fifteenth Army's initial assault gave the Japanese a clear psychological dominance over their opponents, following the capture of their first major objective at Moulmein. Most British, Indian and Burmese soldiers quickly and quite erroneously concluded that the Japanese soldier was somehow a 'superman', highly trained and well prepared for fighting on a jungle battlefield, and who terrifyingly often displayed so-called 'fanatical' bravery in combat and a shocking disdain for his own and prisoners' lives. The initiative now rested firmly in Japanese hands. On 8 February, Fifteenth Army crossed the Salween River, with 33rd Division (which had initially advanced behind its sister formation) crossing near Pa-an in the north and the 55th Division in the south just north of Martaban, with instructions to advance westwards astride the road and railway line to the Bilin River. Both achieved local superiority against 17th Indian Division's forward troops. Fierce fighting occurred at Kuzeik, near the ferry crossing to Pa-an, on 11 February where the Japanese II./215th Regiment overwhelmed the isolated VII./10th Baluch Regiment, with only a handful of Allied officers and men escaping through the jungle. The III./7th Gurkha Rifles, garrisoning Martaban, was briefly cut off, but eventually fought its way clear to safety. A counter-attack in strength by the recently deployed 46th Indian Infantry Brigade failed to materialize. Under heavy pressure, and with 46th Indian Infantry Brigade apparently now being outflanked to the north, the badly over-extended 17th Indian Division withdrew further westwards. Despite repeated pleas from the GOC 17th Indian Division for an immediate withdrawal behind the Sittang River, permission was denied by the headquarters of Burma Army, which was firmly convinced on strategic grounds that a forward defence was vital to hold Rangoon and its key port.

The 17th Indian Division trekked westwards in the face of the advancing Japanese, with orders from Lieutenant-General Tom Hutton, GOC Burma Army, to fight a delaying action along the Thaton–Duyinzeik line for as long as possible. On 14 February, however, Smyth acted on his own responsibility by ordering a further retreat to the Bilin River, fearing that Japanese troops were moving past his division's northern flank through the jungle. The 15-mile-long defensive position at the Bilin River – running along the line of its wide, largely dry or easily fordable, riverbed – on paper at least afforded good fields of fire and an opportunity for 17th Indian Division to concentrate and fight a defensive battle in depth, at a bottleneck where the road and railway from Martaban ran between the estuary to the south and the jungle-covered hills to the north. The 16th Indian Infantry Brigade, reinforced by two extra infantry battalions and two mountain artillery batteries, started occupying defensive positions along the Bilin River on 16 February, while the fresh 48th Indian Infantry Brigade deployed behind it in depth. The 46th Indian Infantry Brigade went into divisional reserve at Kyaikto. The Japanese had stolen a march over their opponents, however, with two regiments from 33rd Division having already reached the river. A composite company had crossed the Bilin River near Ahonwa on the night of 14/15 February, with the Japanese I./214th Regiment wading over and digging in on the western bank

The Indian crew of a heavily camouflaged Bofors anti-aircraft gun await orders before going into battle. (AirSeaLand)

the following day before the British had fully deployed. The 55th Division advanced comparatively slowly westwards along the road and railway line following the capture of Martaban, meanwhile, with its 143rd Regiment moving southwards towards the coast with the intention of crossing the estuary and outflanking the British defences running along the Bilin River from the south. The surprise discovery of Japanese troops already across the river dug in at Danyingon-Paya, by the 2nd King's Own Yorkshire Light Infantry early on 16 February, prompted an immediate unsuccessful attempt to clear the village. A single infantry company, however, reached Yinon further north and dug in. A fierce counter-attack by I./7th Gurkha Rifles at 0800hrs the next morning involving hand-to-hand fighting was unable to dislodge the Japanese, who had also built a small roadblock on the Yinon road south of Paya. A further attempt by the I./4th Gurkha Rifles at 1730hrs proved partially successful, but the Japanese still clung to a shallow bridgehead on the western side of the river. The withdrawal of the V./17th Dogra Regiment, holding outposts on the eastern bank screening the road and railway bridges over the Bilin River, back into reserve, ordered at 1300hrs on 17 February went badly: the battalion virtually collapsed following a clash with the Japanese 215th Regiment that had just arrived in the southern sector. The 16th Indian Infantry Brigade was 'fought to a standstill' over the following days during a series of attacks against the Japanese 214th Regiment, despite strong artillery and RAF support.

The headquarters of 48th Indian Infantry Brigade took over the southern sector of the Bilin defences on 17 February, taking the 1st Royal Jat Regiment, 8th Burma Rifles and remnants of the V./17th Dogras, in addition to its own II./5th Royal Gurkha Rifles under command. The Japanese II./215th Regiment crossed the river near Bilin village on the night of 17/18 February, with the 8th Burma Rifles giving ground and opening a hole in the defensive line. A furious counter-attack by the 5th Royal Gurkha Rifles, however, ejected the Japanese and restored the position. Unknown to the defenders, on 19 February the Japanese 215th Regiment, leaving behind a small detachment to occupy the defenders' attention, moved northwards to reinforce the 214th Regiment on the right flank of the British defensive position. Early on 18 February, reports arrived at brigade headquarters, moreover, that other Japanese troops had landed in strength on the coast at Zokali, threatening the brigade's right flank from the south.

The 17th Indian Division had fought well at the Bilin River, having succeeded in checking the enemy advance and forcing Fifteenth Army to fully deploy its leading division. It was clear the fighting had reached a critical point by 18 February, with the Japanese having outflanked the British defences in strength to the north and south exposing 17th Indian Division's line of retreat if it stayed in place. With his last reserve – the IV./12th Frontier Force Regiment – committed to a counter-attack towards Paya and having lost 350 killed, wounded or missing, Major-General Smyth requested permission at 1645hrs on 18 February to withdraw, which was granted by Hutton the following day when he visited Smyth at Kyaikto. It was not a moment too soon. The leading elements of the Japanese 143rd Regiment had moved quickly inland from the coast, and by early afternoon on 19 February were close by Taungzan railway station and had occupied Taungale near the Bilin Rubber Estate, several miles deep behind the right flank of the crumbling British front line. To meet this unexpected threat, a rifle company

The Battle of the Bilin River, 17–20 February 1942

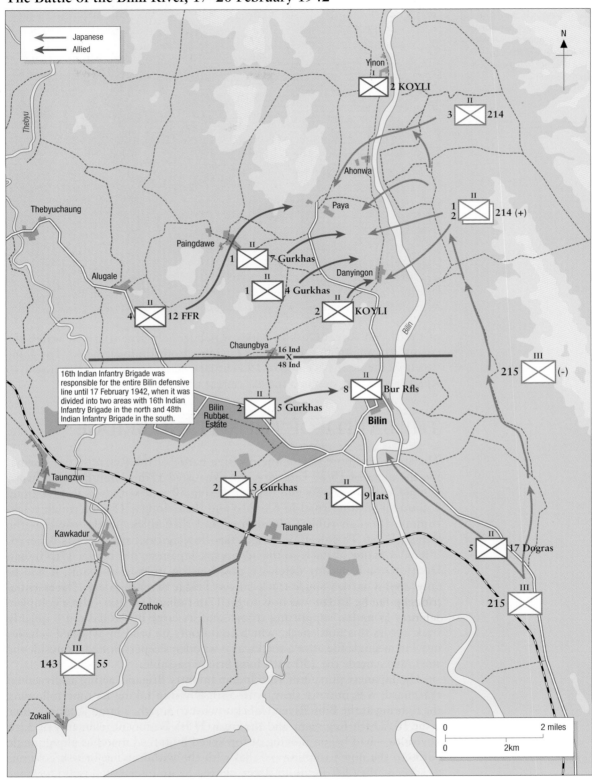

16th Indian Infantry Brigade was responsible for the entire Bilin defensive line until 17 February 1942, when it was divided into two areas with 16th Indian Infantry Brigade in the north and 48th Indian Infantry Brigade in the south.

The hardy pack mule often provided the only means of transportation in the dense Burmese jungle, where roads or tracks suitable for wheeled vehicles were marked by their absence. (Mcdaniel/AP/Shutterstock)

of the II./5th Royal Gurkha Rifles was hurriedly sent south to watch the enemy, but an attempt to eject the Japanese from Taungale failed. The game was up. Late on the evening of 19 February, Smyth ordered a withdrawal to Kyaikto as a first step in a further retreat to the Sittang River.

THE BATTLE OF THE SITTANG BRIDGE

The stage was now set for the decisive battle of the Retreat from Burma. On the night of 19/20 February, the exhausted 17th Indian Division broke contact with the enemy and began a taxing 30-mile withdrawal, first along a good all-weather road to Kyaikto and then along a 15-mile rough track, running through rubber plantations and then thick jungle, towards the Sittang River. This deep, wide and fast-flowing tidal river, it was believed, offered a major obstacle to the advancing Japanese, but before 17th Indian Division could occupy defensive positions on its western bank, it had to cross over a narrow single-track railway bridge to reach safety. The essential problem facing Smyth was how to get 17th Indian Division – three complete infantry brigades, supporting troops and its large divisional tail – quickly back across this bottleneck, which could only be used by wheeled vehicles moving in single file after a trackway – wooden sleepers bolted alongside the steel rails – made the 550-yard-long bridge passable.

The Japanese pursuit of 48th Indian Infantry Brigade, acting as divisional rearguard, was initially slow, with 55th Division taking its time following the fighting at the Bilin River. Unbeknownst to Smyth, a large Japanese force – the III./214th Regiment and the fresh 215th Regiment (elements of 33rd Division) – had begun moving at top speed by forced marches along jungle paths to the north running parallel with the withdrawing British columns as soon as they left the Bilin River, alerted by an intercepted radio message saying a withdrawal was under way. By the end of 20 February, the two leading brigades, exhausted after the four-day battle at the Bilin River, having broken contact and then marching 15 miles, had reached the Boyagi Rubber Estate/Kyaikto area halfway to the bridge where the all-weather road stopped.

The route chosen by Major-General Smyth for the next stage of the withdrawal followed an unmetalled rough track, running in the middle of a 40-yard-wide trace cut through jungle (following the alignment of a yet-to-be-built metalled road), with small detachments posted to the north and along the railway line to the south providing flank protection (the latter had been judged too vulnerable to seaborne attack to be used). Late in the evening of 20 February, Smyth ordered the IV./12th Frontier Force Regiment and Malerkotla Sappers to reinforce the Sittang bridgehead on the eastern bank of the river early the following day. Its close defence was entrusted just to the weak 3rd Burma Rifles, despite Brigadier Roger Ekin's strong recommendation to deploy a full brigade to defend the bridgehead and send back the divisional transport.

The 17th Indian Division's physically and mentally exhausted men spent a fitful and disturbed night of 20/21 February at Kyaikto, with Japanese patrols firing intermittently into bivouacs overnight, and at 0500hrs the following morning the divisional headquarters was attacked by a raiding party. The IV./12th Frontier Force Regiment and Malerkotlas departed aboard lorries to the bridge early that morning, with divisional headquarters followed in turn by 48th Indian Infantry Brigade travelling the same route towards the Sittang, before halting overnight at Mokpalin Quarries and crossing the bridge the next day. Major-General Smyth and the divisional headquarters left at 1000hrs, followed by the 48th Indian Brigade an hour later at 1100hrs and other divisional troops, whose combined vehicles and pack transport filled the available road space. The extremely slow pace of the withdrawal by the exhausted British, Indian, Gurkha and Burmese troops (according to some showing an appalling lack of urgency), was hampered by the intense

Japanese infantry cross a river in Burma using an improvised footbridge built beside the original bridge demolished by Indian sappers. (Gamma-Keystone via Getty Images)

heat, clouds of billowing white dust, water shortages and the capacity of the poor track running first through paddy and then dense jungle. Further delays and disorganization were caused by bombing and strafing attacks by 'friendly' RAF Hurricanes and Blenheims and AVG P-40 Tomahawks on the withdrawing columns, mistaking them for the Japanese, which caused casualties amongst men and pack animals, wrecked vehicles and perhaps most significantly destroyed many radios upon which command and control of the division depended.

The Japanese had made rapid progress towards the Sittang River, moving cross-country along rough jungle tracks lying a few miles to the north of the route being used by British Commonwealth troops. A detachment of 2nd Burma Frontier Force, covering the northern approaches to the Sittang Bridge at Kinmun, clashed with the leading elements of the Japanese I./215th Regiment during the afternoon of 21 February, before withdrawing northwards and escaping across the Sittang River by boat. News of the advancing Japanese columns reached divisional HQ late that evening. By dusk, only the IV./12th Frontier Force Regiment had arrived at the bridge to reinforce the 250-strong 3rd Burma Rifles already deployed on Buddha Hill (a high point crowned by a large statue of Buddha) on a 500-yard-long, low ridge running adjacent to the eastern end of the bridge. Overnight, the Malerkotla Field Company worked with a will preparing the central three spans of the railway bridge for demolition, while the 24th Field Company RE on the western bank began destroying all civilian boats that had been gathered upriver, to deny them to the enemy. The divisional headquarters and 48th Indian Infantry Brigade, which had left the Boyagyi Estate at 1100hrs on 21 February, and its leading battalion – the I./4th Gurkha Rifles – reached the Mokpalin Quarries at 1730hrs that evening along with the brigade HQ, after a hot, dusty and exhausting march; the rest of the brigade (the II./5th Royal Gurkha Rifles and the I./3rd Gurkha Rifles) bivouacked where water

A British NCO instructs his men how to employ a .303 Bren light machine gun on a tripod anti-aircraft mount. The Bren gun was one of the finest infantry weapons in British service. (AirSeaLand)

was available further back down the road. The road between the bridge and Mokpalin village was now jammed with the massed divisional motor transport, which only began crossing the bridge at 0200hrs on 22 February after the roadway for vehicles was finally completed.

The morning of 22 February dawned bright and clear at the Sittang River, with long lines of cars, lorries, ambulances and other assorted vehicles still awaiting their turn to cross the bridge, which the Malerkotla Field Company reported at 0600hrs ready for demolition. Following receipt of a warning from Army HQ at Rangoon that a Japanese parachute landing was imminent on the western side of the river, at 0400hrs the I./4th Gurkha Rifles quickly crossed to reinforce the defences, where it took a detached company of the 2nd Duke of Wellington's Regiment under command. A blockage – caused when a three-ton Officers' Mess truck came off the roadway and became jammed between two steel girders – added a further two-hour delay until 0630hrs, and shortly afterwards both the divisional and 48th Indian Brigade headquarters crossed the bridge. The rest of 17th Indian Division was still miles away from the Sittang River early on 22 February, with divisional headquarters having badly underestimated the time needed to reach the bridge and for the queuing divisional transport to cross. The 16th Indian Infantry had spent 21 February resting at Boyagyi Estate as planned, under periodic attack by marauding Japanese aircraft, while 46th Indian Infantry Brigade, now acting as rearguard, remained in place along the Kadat Chaung near Kyaikto, to the acute consternation of both brigade commanders who by evening wanted to immediately move to the bridge. At 0100hrs on 22 February, both brigades were finally warned by divisional headquarters that the Japanese were moving around the northern flank of the division and that they should move towards the Sittang River as quickly as possible.

The Japanese advance guard – the I./215th Regiment and supporting artillery and engineers – reached Pyinkadogon in the early hours of 22 February, five miles short of the Sittang. At 0830hrs, it broke cover and seized Sittang village upstream of the bridge, putting the motor ferry out of action, before capturing Buddha Hill at the eastern end of the low ridge that commanded the bridge and its approaches from the surprised 3rd Burma Rifles. A foothold was also secured by the Japanese on nearby Pagoda Hill at the western end of the ridge, but crucially an attempt to rush the railway bridge was thwarted. The IV./12th Frontier Force Regiment, which had planned to take up defensive positions on the ridge that morning, supported by the weak VII./10th Baluch Regiment, launched an immediate fierce counter-attack that threw the Japanese back from Pagoda Hill in disorder, but the enemy remained firmly entrenched on nearby Buddha Hill where they were steadily reinforced. Further Japanese attacks were made on the motor transport jammed closely together on the road south of Mokpalin. The Officer Commanding (OC) 48th Indian Infantry Brigade, Brigadier Noel Hugh-Jones, was given command at 1000hrs of all troops within the bridgehead, including the IV./12th Frontier Force Regiment on Buddha Hill; D Company, the 2nd Duke of Wellington's Regiment on Bungalow Hill; and the remnants of the 3rd Burma Rifles and VII./10th Baluch Regiment near the riverbank. The II./5th Royal Gurkha Rifles followed by the I./3rd Gurkha Rifles, meanwhile, secured Mokpalin and the divisional transport from Japanese attacks by occupying the high ground on the eastern side of the road, including Outpost Hill, beyond which a ravine ran along the base of the southern slopes of Pagoda and Buddha hills. Little was known of

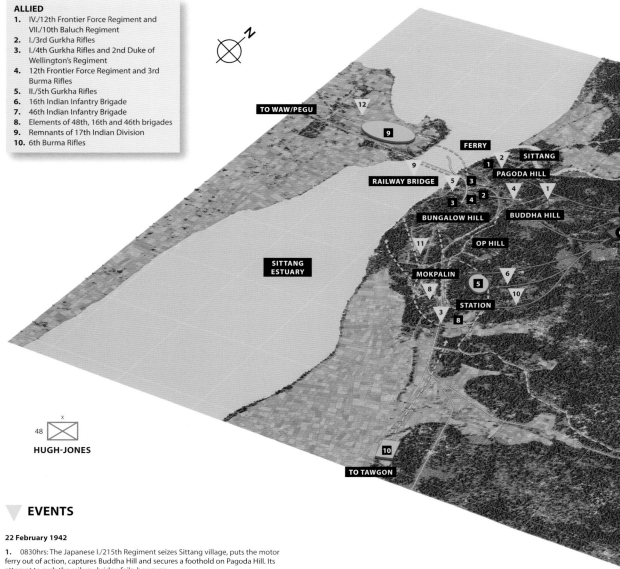

TO WAW/PEGU

FERRY

SITTANG

PAGODA HILL

RAILWAY BRIDGE

BUNGALOW HILL

BUDDHA HILL

OP HILL

SITTANG ESTUARY

MOKPALIN

STATION

48 X

HUGH-JONES

TO TAWGON

EVENTS

22 February 1942

1. 0830hrs: The Japanese I./215th Regiment seizes Sittang village, puts the motor ferry out of action, captures Buddha Hill and secures a foothold on Pagoda Hill. Its attempt to rush the railway bridge fails, however.

2. c.0900hrs: IV./12th Frontier Force Regiment and VII./10th Baluch Regiment (less elements) counter-attack and throw the Japanese back from Pagoda Hill.

3. Morning: Japanese attacks on the motor transport jammed closely together on the road south of Mokpalin continue.

4. 1400hrs: After a fierce bombardment of Buddha and Pagoda hills by two mountain batteries, I./3rd Gurkha Rifles assault and secure Buddha Hill with heavy losses.

5. 1530hrs: I./4th Gurkha Rifles and 2nd Duke of Wellington's Regiment are sent back across the river and re-occupy their positions between Pagoda Hill and Bungalow Hill. The 12th Frontier Force Regiment and 3rd Burma Rifles form an inner perimeter behind the ridge.

6. Japanese exert heavy pressure on II./5th Gurkha Rifles on the north-east flank of Mokpalin.

7. Afternoon: 16th Indian Infantry Brigade reaches Mokaplin Quarries largely without interference. The rearguard 46th Indian Infantry Brigade is ambushed by the Japanese III./124th Infantry in a patch of dense jungle; its column splits up amidst the ensuing confusion.

8. Evening: The now mixed-up elements of 48th, 16th and 46th brigades form a perimeter camp around Mokpalin. The camp comes under heavy attack as darkness falls.

23 February 1942

9. 0520hrs: After the Allied troops holding the bridgehead are evacuated to safety, the Sittang Bridge is demolished to avoid it falling into Japanese hands. A substantial part of 17th Indian Division remains on the eastern bank of the river.

10. Morning: Several Japanese attempts to capture Mokpalin, supported by mortars, artillery and bombers, are beaten off.

11. 1400hrs: Jones orders his shaken troops to withdraw to the riverbank. Weapons, equipment and clothing are abandoned and men attempt to swim the river or cross aboard hastily built rafts. Many drown. Others escape into the jungle and later cross the Sittang further north, while 300 use a hurriedly made lifeline thrown over the gap made in the bridge to escape. Many east of the river are captured.

12. The remnants of 17th Indian Division withdraw to Pegu.

SITTANG BRIDGE, 22–23 FEBRUARY 1942

The Battle of the Sittang Bridge proved the decisive engagement of the invasion of Burma, with the loss of a large part of 17th Indian Division effectively destroying British hopes of defending Rangoon and, with it, of holding lower Burma.

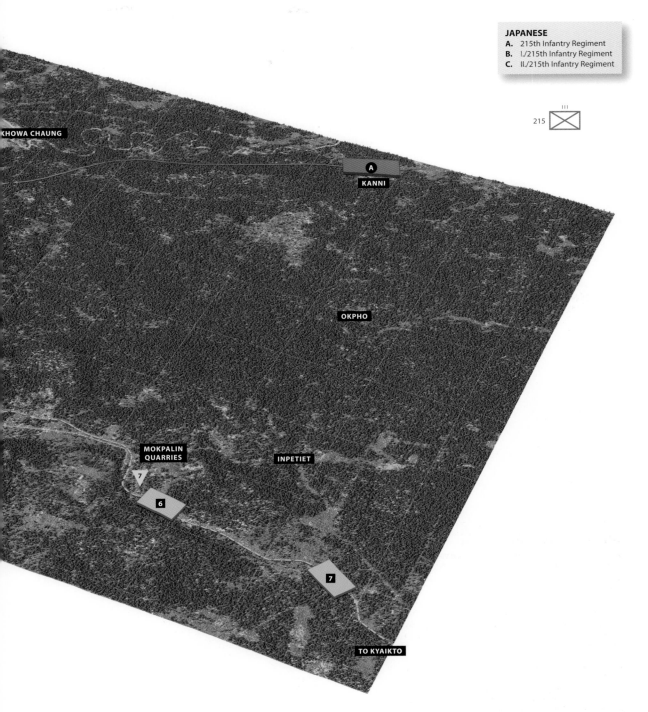

JAPANESE
A. 215th Infantry Regiment
B. I./215th Infantry Regiment
C. II./215th Infantry Regiment

215

KHOWA CHAUNG

A
KANNI

OKPHO

MOKPALIN
QUARRIES

INPETIET

7

6

7

TO KYAIKTO

Note: gridlines are shown at intervals of 1km (0.62 miles)

other British positions east of the river, however, by higher command due to a breakdown in communications. Following a fierce bombardment of Buddha and Pagoda hills by two mountain batteries, the I./3rd Gurkha Rifles assaulted the ridge at 1400hrs, and after bitter fighting secured Buddha Hill despite heavy losses. This 'friendly' heavy barrage had unintended consequences, however: the heavy casualties it and intermittent Japanese shellfire inflicted upon bridgehead troops holding Pagoda Hill (whose position was unknown to the gunners) convinced Brigadier Noel Hugh-Jones to withdraw his men across the river and to hold the position by fire alone. A second Japanese attempt to seize the bridge later that day was beaten back by the remnants of the I./3rd Gurkha Rifles, who retained control of Buddha Hill during the afternoon. At 1530hrs, Smyth sent the I./4th Gurkha Rifles and 2nd Dukes back across the river, where they reoccupied their positions from Pagoda Hill to Bungalow Hill, while the 12th Frontier Force Regiment and 3rd Burma Rifles formed an inner perimeter behind the ridge. Heavy pressure was also exerted on II./5th Gurkha Rifles that afternoon on the north-east flank of Mokpalin.

The main body of 17th Indian Division moved towards the Sittang River on 22 February, now that the bridge was open to traffic and the rough track ahead to Mokpalin had cleared of other vehicles. The 16th Indian Infantry Brigade left Boyagyi Estate at 0600hrs, and making slow progress along the rough track reached Mokpalin Quarries – two to three miles from the bridge – in the afternoon, largely without interference. Unfortunately, a gap had opened up between it and the rearguard – 46th Indian Infantry Brigade – which was ambushed by the Japanese III./124th Infantry where the track ran through a patch of dense jungle. Heavy

An Indian crew hurriedly reassemble their dismantled QF 3.7in. howitzer weapon and bring it into action. This highly effective weapon was normally broken down into eight loads, and could be transported by mules anywhere men could march on foot. (AirSeaLand)

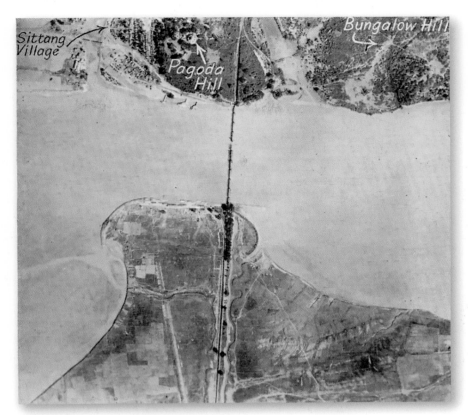

Sittang Village

Pagoda Hill

Bungalow Hill

This annotated aerial photograph of the Sittang Bridge and its immediate environs clearly shows several key terrain features and a wide gap in the bridge caused when the Malerkotla Sappers demolished several spans. (Public domain)

fighting ensued to clear an enemy roadblock – made of hastily felled trees – and to make further progress towards the river. The 46th Indian Brigade's column split up amidst the ensuing confusion and marched along the track or through the jungle towards the bridge. Unaware of the exact situation at the Sittang Bridge and still out of contact with divisional headquarters, Brigadier Jones at Mokpalin immediately ordered Outpost Hill be held in strength, and overnight the now mixed-up elements of 48th, 16th and 46th brigades formed a perimeter camp around Mokpalin. This position came under heavy attack as darkness fell, with mortar fire destroying many parked vehicles still crowding the road. A provisional plan to attack towards Buddha and Pagoda hills, believed to be in enemy hands, was hatched for the next morning.

The fog of war cloaked the bridgehead over the Sittang River during the night of 22/23 February, with an exhausted and badly stressed Brigadier Noel Hugh-Jones unable to make contact with the headquarters of either 16th Indian Infantry Brigade or 46th Indian Infantry Brigade east of the river, which he believed were incapable of fighting through to safety. Only a handful of officers and men, cut off from their units, from either formation had reached the bridge through the jungle to tell what had happened, and inexplicably no attempts were made to establish contact by sending out patrols, despite their comrades being only hundreds of yards away in the jungle. At 0200hrs, Brigadier Hugh-Jones, under strict orders that the bridge should not fall into enemy hands, asked Major Richard Orgill, who commanded the Malerkotla Sappers, whether the demolition of the bridge could be guaranteed if the structure came under direct fire at daylight. With Japanese machine-gun bullets already ricocheting off the steel girders and threatening the lives of

his sappers, it was impossible for him to give such an assurance. Following a brief conference with his battalion commanders, Hugh-Jones – convinced the bridgehead would collapse if heavily attacked at dawn, and that, if demolition was impossible in daylight, the bridge would fall into Japanese hands – requested permission to destroy the bridge from the divisional commander. After reflecting on the situation, Major-General Smyth took the 'ghastly' decision and authorized Brigadier Hugh-Jones to destroy the bridge at a time of his own choosing. At 0520hrs on the morning of 23 February 1942, after the troops holding the bridgehead were evacuated to safety, the Sittang Bridge was demolished. A substantial part of 17th Indian Division that still remained on the eastern bank of the river heard three massive detonations, as two spans of the bridge plunged into the river below and a third was badly damaged.

The shocked officers and men in 16th Indian Infantry Brigade and 46th Indian Infantry Brigade cut off from escape on the eastern bank of the river in and around Mokpalin had little time to take stock during a brief period of quiet that spread across the battlefield following the shattering explosions marking the destruction of the railway bridge. A planned attack on Buddha and Pagoda hills was immediately cancelled and orders issued to hold firm in place until darkness fell. Several Japanese attempts to capture Mokpalin, supported by mortars, artillery and bombers, that morning were beaten off, following which, at 1400hrs, Jones ordered his shaken troops to withdraw to the riverbank, where a low cliff provided some protection from enemy fire. Confusion reigned as weapons, equipment and clothing were hurriedly abandoned and already exhausted men took to the water in search of escape, either by swimming the mile-wide, fast-flowing Sittang River or crossing aboard hastily built rafts. Many drowned making the attempt. Some reluctant to risk the water escaped into the jungle and later crossed the Sittang further north, while 300 used a hurriedly made lifeline thrown over the gap in the bridge to escape. Many non-swimmers and seriously wounded unable to escape went into Japanese captivity, as did those holding off the enemy on the southern side of the Mokpalin perimeter who had missed the order to withdraw.

The Battle of the Sittang Bridge proved the decisive engagement of the invasion of Burma in 1942, with the loss of a large part of 17th Indian Division effectively destroying British hopes of defending Rangoon, and, with it, of holding lower Burma. The remnants of 17th Indian Division,

A new greatly enlarged pagoda, incorporating the original structure, stands on the site of the fierce fighting that occurred near the Sittang Bridge in February 1942 between 17th Indian Division and its Japanese opponents. (© Mary Cole)

having lost many artillery pieces and most of its transport and equipment, withdrew to Pegu, where a roll call held on 24 February revealed its infantry units only mustered 80 officers and 3,403 Other Ranks (with 1,420 rifles between them). The 17th Indian Division was now clearly incapable of halting a Japanese advance on Rangoon, even after being rested, reorganized, re-equipped at Pegu and reinforced by the leading elements of 7th Armoured Brigade that on 21 February disembarked at the port and was rushed to the front. A shameless search for a scapegoat quickly began that has continued until the present day, with Major-General John Smyth's actions at every stage of the battle being second-guessed by historians picking over discrepancies in differing accounts of the affair. A seriously ill Smyth was humiliatingly sacked by Wavell on 1 March at divisional headquarters at Hlegu, but his replacement – Major-General David 'Punch' Cowan (formerly Smyth's GSOI) – had been dealt an impossible hand.

THE TAUKKYAN–PROME ROADBLOCK, 1500HRS, 7 MARCH 1942 (PP. 50–51)

Shown here are the Japanese defenders (**1**) occupying part of a hastily improvised roadblock (**2**) on the Taukkyan to Prome road. Down the road ahead of them is an attacking Bren Gun carrier (**3**) accompanied by officers and men of the 1st Gloucesters (**4**), who are making an initial 'hasty' attack on the position. The attackers are coming under heavy fire from the roadblock and surrounding jungle – snipers and machine guns hidden in the trees – and have gone to ground.

The blocking position on the road, located near Satthwadaw, was protecting the flank of the Japanese 33rd Division, which was preventing the Allied Rangoon garrison making good its escape. This hurriedly built roadblock itself consists of branches and tree trunks hastily piled on the road to create an obstacle and provide cover for the defenders. The Japanese infantrymen are supported by the gun crew of a 75mm Type 41 Mountain Gun (**5**), part of III./214th Regiment. Three-inch mortar rounds are detonating in and around the roadblock (**6**).

A knocked-out Indian Pattern wheeled carrier (**7**), with a damaged right front wheel, has slid sideways into the wide drainage ditch ahead of the roadblock.

The British soldiers of the 1st Gloucesters are armed with Lee-Enfield rifles with bayonets fixed. An M3 Stuart light tank (**8**) from 7th Hussars can also be seen behind the Bren carrier.

THE FALL OF RANGOON AND THE TAUKKYAN ROADBLOCK

The initiative now rested firmly with the Imperial Japanese Army, which it kept largely undisputed for the rest of the invasion of Burma. Fifteenth Army's leading units crossed the Sittang River by ferry or small boats at Kunzeik, north of the demolished railway bridge, in late February, with the main body of 55th Division crossing the river on 3–4 March with orders to capture Pegu. The 33rd Division followed in its wake with instructions to move largely undetected westwards through the jungle-clad hills to cut the Rangoon–Prome road, before swinging southwards down the railway line and capturing the port that Lieutenant-General Iida believed would be defended by Burma Army to the last man and round. The II./143rd Regiment provided flank protection in the Sittang valley, while another detached battalion advanced south-west towards the Syriam oil refineries.

The British 7th Armoured Brigade, commanded by Brigadier John Anstice, had been quickly thrown into battle at Waw north-east of Rangoon (bolstered by the fresh 1st West Yorkshires and 1st Cameronians), providing a protective screen behind which the battered 17th Indian Division could rest and reorganize at Pegu and Hlegu, with a small detached force actively patrolling the vital road running north from Rangoon to Prome in the Irrawaddy valley. This confident, highly experienced and well-trained armoured formation – fresh from fighting German and Italian troops in the Western Desert as part of the famous 7th Armoured Division – played a vital role throughout the rest of the campaign. The Stuart light tank quickly proved itself as a source of invaluable close support for the hard-pressed infantry during early clashes between patrols, that the Japanese were unable to knock out except by attacks from close quarters with petrol bombs or mines and fire from larger-calibre artillery. Efforts to rebuild a practicable defensive line running between Pegu and the Sittang, however, quickly failed after the Japanese crossed the Sittang River in strength, and the defence focussed instead on the small town of Pegu, defended by 48th Indian Infantry Brigade, lying further to the west of Waw. Further British reinforcements, meanwhile, had hurriedly landed at Rangoon, which fortunately had been spared further air raids since those on 25/26 February, largely because the Japanese wished to capture the port intact. The 1st Indian Field Regiment

A crowd of Burmese onlookers pose beside a Japanese fighter downed during an air raid on Rangoon. (AirSeaLand)

The Fall of Rangoon, March 1942

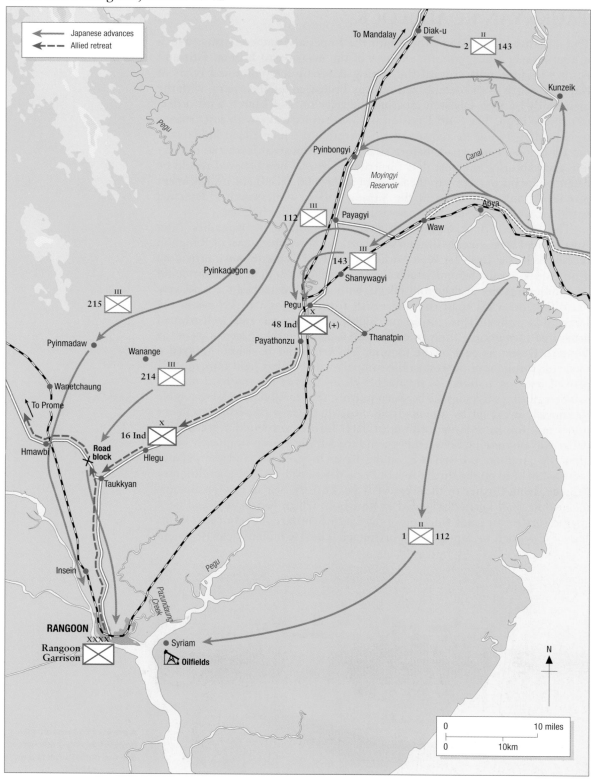

arrived on 3 March, equipped with 16 25pdr field guns, providing Burma Army with a source of much-needed artillery firepower; and two days later, 63rd Indian Infantry Brigade, commanded by Brigadier John Wickham, landed at the deserted docks. It was the last major reinforcement to reach Burma Army, but like its predecessors it consisted primarily of raw and badly trained Indian recruits. Calamity struck almost immediately when the brigade commander and all three battalion COs were killed or badly wounded in a BIA ambush returning from a reconnaissance trip to Pegu. The fervent hope that the battle-hardened 7th Australian Division would land at Rangoon at the last moment proved an illusion, with the defence of its homeland understandably proving more important to the Australian government. Although General Sir Harold Alexander, who had replaced Hutton as GOC Burma Army on 5 March, initially agreed with Wavell that the British could hold the port, the opposite quickly became clear as events took a dramatic turn for the worse.

The Japanese 55th Division moved quickly through the wooded low hills lying to the north of Pegu after crossing the Sittang River, to launch a surprise attack on the town. The Japanese 143rd Regiment was tasked with assaulting the built-up area from the west, while the III./112th Regiment swung round and built a roadblock on the southwards road to Hlegu. Japanese plans to counter British armour using anti-tank weapons specially brought to Pegu did not go to plan. Early in the misty morning of 6 March, a troop of the 3rd Hussars patrolling the Pegu road was ambushed by a Japanese anti-tank battery. The latter's 37mm AP shells proved incapable of penetrating their armour and only succeeded in blowing the tracks off several tanks. A spirited counter-attack by tanks and the 1st West Yorkshires captured all four guns, and shortly afterwards three totally outclassed Type 95 Ha-Go light tanks (a platoon detached from 2nd Tank Regiment) were destroyed during a very brief tank versus tank engagement. The Japanese 143rd Regiment achieved surprise and rapidly captured the town and railway station during the early morning from the initially shocked defenders, who

Japanese troops entering Rangoon station in January 1942. (© Imperial War Museum, HU 2773)

Japanese infantry enter Rangoon following its capture, with the huge Shwedagon Pagoda visible in the background. (Public domain)

had wrongly anticipated an attack from the north and east, before being forcibly ejected from the part of Pegu near the Hlegu road by a fierce counter-attack at midday carried out at the point of the bayonet. The strength and ferocity of the Japanese thrust towards Rangoon via Pegu and impossibility of mounting a strong counter-attack quickly convinced General Alexander to reverse his earlier decision made on 3 March to hold the embattled town at all costs (which itself had reversed a decision by Hutton to evacuate Pegu). A withdrawal from the burning town, subjected to repeated Japanese air raids throughout the day, was ordered at 2000hrs on 6 March, with the hard-pressed defenders accompanied by its 190 vehicles to withdraw early the following morning southwards down the road towards Hlegu. The leading Stuarts of the 3rd Hussars blasted their way through the roadblock near Payathonzu at 0830hrs, consisting of two wrecked lorries lying nose to nose across the road, and proceeded onwards to Hlegu with their second-line transport and supporting artillery battery following closely behind. A single tank was lost to a petrol bomb. Unfortunately, the main column had lagged behind the 3rd Hussars, having come under heavy attack from both sides of the road after leaving the blazing town. The Japanese had reoccupied the position by the time the leading I./7th Gurkha Rifles had reached the roadblock, after the main column had forced the enemy back on either flank and the advance resumed. The initial attempt to force the roadblock failed with heavy loss, and it took a further assault and several hours before the badly battered Japanese withdrew northwards to safety and the road reopened to traffic. The 48th Indian Infantry Brigade eventually reached Hlegu at 1300hrs, where its depleted infantry battalions were picked up by lorries.

The loss of Pegu meant in turn a protracted defence of the Burmese capital was clearly impossible, with its defenders now in serious danger of being cut off. On the evening of 7 March, the Rangoon garrison withdrew northwards from the largely empty city, where law and order had broken down, to escape encirclement. Soon after, it joined up with the troops of 17th Indian Division and 7th Armoured Brigade withdrawing from Pegu. A small band of intrepid sappers and sailors, left behind in Rangoon to complete the demolition of port facilities, warehouses packed full of Lend Lease equipment and other vital installations to deny them to the enemy, were the very last to leave the port. These 'last ditchers' were carried downriver in launches to waiting merchant ships past the Burmah Oil Company's blazing Syriam oil refineries, tank farms and pumping houses demolished or set afire the day before. Some 21 miles north of the city at Satthwadaw the combined column – over 1,000 tanks, armoured cars, lorries and other assorted vehicles in a massive column stretching 40 miles – was brought to a sudden halt by a roadblock hurriedly built by the Japanese III./214th Regiment, just after the advanced guard had passed by en route to Tharrawaddy. Burma Army was now bottled up in a trap, and its complete destruction was now a distinct possibility. A series of increasingly desperate piecemeal attacks were mounted using Stuart light tanks, Bren gun carriers and infantry; these were beaten off by the Japanese, who had deployed infantry, machine guns and regimental guns in and around the roadblock, made of felled trees and later reinforced with tar barrels, forcing the column to halt overnight strung out down the road. It appeared the loss of the entire Burma Army was now at hand if the escape route from Rangoon could not be cleared, and orders were issued for the force to split up into parties of 12 men and escape to India, if the block was not cleared by an attack the next morning. The 63rd Indian Infantry Brigade, following a brief artillery bombardment, moved forward the following morning with tank support, to discover the roadblock had been abandoned overnight, whose defenders, mindful of their orders just to shield 33rd Division's crossing of the road and then capture Rangoon, had left. The column escaped northwards towards Tharrawaddy and safety without being subjected to air attack or close pursuit. On 8 March, to its surprise, the Japanese 33rd Division occupied the abandoned city, isolating Burma Army from outside support, cutting the Burma Road and opening the port to further enemy reinforcements from Japan, Indo-China and those freed following the end of the Malayan campaign. In comparison, Burma Army was a wasting asset, diminishing in strength every day from enemy action, disease and desertion, without hope of major reinforcement or re-equipment and nearly completely dependent on backloaded stocks of food, ammunition and other supplies hastily evacuated from Rangoon by road, river and train and for petrol on the oilfields and refineries at Yenangyaung.

Oil installations on the Rangoon waterfront ablaze in March 1942. When the Allies realized the Japanese advance towards Rangoon could not be halted, a 'scorched earth' programme was implemented to deny its oil supplies to the enemy. The fire from this particular depot burned for six weeks. (Northcliffe Collection/ANL/Shutterstock)

BATTLE AT SHWEGYIN, 11 MARCH 1942 (PP. 58–59)

The attack on Shwegyin carried out by 2nd Burma Brigade was part of a larger attack by 1st Burdiv southwards from Nyaunglebin timed to coincided with an offensive by 17th Indian Division towards Prome (which failed to happen). On 11 March, 2nd Burma Brigade – V./1st Punjab Regiment, VII./Burma Rifles and 3rd Frontier Force (a Burma Frontier Force column) – attacked southwards and seized Madauk, before crossing the Sittang River to take Shwegyin on the eastern bank. It encountered heavy resistance at the latter from BIA troops and a handful of Japanese soldiers who fought hard, hiding in houses, culverts and up trees until they withdrew. It proved a short-lived victory, however, and soon after it withdrew from the briefly re-captured town. According to the regimental history, this action was the baptism of fire for the V./1st Punjab Regiment in Burma.

Shown here are Indian infantry (**1**) – bearded Sikhs from V./1st Punjab Regiment – carrying out an attack on Japanese positions (**2**) in Shwegyin (just before 1st Burdiv handed over to the Chinese and withdrew to the Irrawaddy valley). A two-man Kumaoni Bren gun team (**3**) from VII./Burma Rifles is firing at the withdrawing Japanese. The turbaned Sikhs have bayonets fixed to Lee-Enfield rifles. A *Havildar* (sergeant, **4**) – stripes visible on his sleeve – is firing a Thompson SMG. A Japanese sniper hidden in a tree (**5**) has been hit. The Japanese soldiers are armed with Type 99 rifles; one is carrying a Nambu LMG by its handle (**6**). The Japanese are wearing tropical uniform, packs and belts with ammunition pouches, puttees and boots.

THE BATTLE FOR CENTRAL BURMA: PROME, TOUNGOO AND YENANGYAUNG

The officers and men of Burma Army enjoyed a long-awaited brief period of rest during the operational pause following the fall of Rangoon, while new plans were quickly devised to defend central Burma and various changes in command and staffs at all levels were carried out. A hastily improvised, understrength and ill-equipped Corps HQ – 1st Burma Corps, or more simply 'Burcorps' – finally arrived from India on 19 March, under the command of General Sir William Slim, who had just arrived in-country after commanding 10th Indian Division in Iraq, with 17th Indian Division, 1st Burma Division and 7th Armoured Brigade under command. Apart from the 1st Inniskilling Fusiliers airlifted into the country on 9 March 1942 by USAAF B-17 bombers, further large-scale reinforcements from India were impossible. Henceforward, Burcorps conducted day-to-day fighting while the HQ of Burma Army, based at Maymyo, was free to concentrate on higher strategic command, political affairs and administration. A further major blow was inflicted upon Burma Army before the end of the month. On 21–22 March the newly formed Burma Wing (Burwing) – reduced to a strength of just 16 Hurricane fighters, nine Blenheim bombers and six AVG P-40 Tomahawks at Magwe and ten Hurricanes at Akyab ten days before – suffered catastrophic further losses when the main airfield at Magwe was raided repeatedly by Japanese fighters and bombers and the runways rendered unusable. A dozen fighters and Blenheim light bombers were wrecked on the ground. The handful of surviving AVG Tomahawks flew north, and the remaining airworthy RAF aircraft withdrew first to Akyab Island and then, after further heavy Japanese air raids, onwards to India, depriving Burma Army of any air support and giving the Japanese complete command of the air over southern and central Burma.

The British high command's plan for defending central Burma from an enemy advance towards Meiktila–Mandalay (the new base area for the

A large group of Japanese air crew carry out a last-minute briefing in front of a line of bombers before mounting operations over southern Burma. (ullstein bild via Getty Images)

Burma Army) and providing security for the Yenangyaung oilfields, had two distinct elements, with the entry of large Chinese Nationalist forces into the country forming an essential part, given the paucity of British Commonwealth 'boots on the ground'. Indeed, without the Chinese Expeditionary Force (CEF), cobbling together a viable defence of central Burma would have been impossible. General Alexander initially hoped to maintain an 80-mile-long front running from Toungoo to Prome, with the jungle-covered Pegu Yoma hills or uplands separating both allies. The badly battered Burcorps – 7th Armoured Brigade, 17th Indian Division and later 1st Burma Division – was deployed in the Irrawaddy valley to block an advance up the river, railway and road northwards from Rangoon. The vital communication centres of Prome and Allanmyo, each garrisoned by a brigade, were fortified and stocked with sufficient supplies to hold out even if bypassed, with mobile forces held in reserve further to the rear to strike back against advancing enemy spearheads. A small force of Royal Marines, Burma Royal Navy Volunteer Reservists and civilians, carried by launches and steamers requisitioned from the Irrawaddy Flotilla Company (known as Force Viper) actively patrolled the Irrawaddy River, as well as landing small demolition and raiding parties of commandos and Royal Marines to wreak havoc behind enemy lines. The newly deployed CEF, under Lieutenant-General Joseph 'Vinegar Joe' Stilwell's command, was given responsibility for blocking the road and railway up the Sittang valley. The Chinese Fifth Army (200th, 22nd and 96th divisions) was tasked with defending Toungoo and covering Mandalay, deploying behind a screen provided by 1st Burma Division at Nyaunglebin before it moved by rail to the Irrawaddy valley, while the Sixth Army (49th, 93rd and 55th divisions) was deployed in the Shan States monitoring the border with Thailand and Indo-China. The very weak Sixty-Sixth Army (New 28th, New 29th and New 38th divisions) provided a reserve.

The unopposed capture of Rangoon came as a major surprise to the Japanese high command and was greeted with jubilation by the men of 33rd Division. This picture of cheering troops was taken in front of the headquarters of the former British Governor of Burma. (GRANGER/Alamy)

The fall of Rangoon on 8 March – a stunning Japanese victory following close on the heels of that achieved at the Sittang River – convinced an exultant Japanese Imperial Headquarters that an advance into upper Burma to Mandalay and then Myitkyina was now practicable. Large-scale reinforcements were despatched from Singapore and Japan to Burma, now the Imperial Japanese Navy had won command of the sea in the Indian Ocean. On 15 March, HQ Fifteenth Army, having rested, reorganized and reinforced its units, issued operational orders for a further advance with the objective of Mandalay and the defeat of Chinese forces entering Burma; the main effort would be made on the right flank in the Sittang valley to cut off a retreat to China. Further reinforcements gradually arrived by sea, including 33rd Division's missing 213th Infantry Regiment and mountain artillery regiment. On 25 March, the motorized 56th Division, commanded by Lieutenant-General Masao Watanabe, landed at Rangoon. It was followed on 7 April by 18th Division, led by Lieutenant-General Renya Mutuguchi, as well as two tank regiments (each equipped with 35 mostly Type 97 Chi-Ha medium tanks) and further artillery, railway, transport and engineer units. Significantly, the latter included the 26th Independent Engineer Regiment equipped with armoured landing barges and motor launches, enabling the Japanese to use the Irrawaddy River to advance into the heart of Burma and freely switch troops between either riverbank. The Japanese 5th Air Division was also reinforced with the 7th and 8th Air brigades, giving it a strength of 420 aircraft.

The well-equipped and highly trained Chinese 200th Division performed extremely well at Toungoo in the Sittang valley, holding up the Japanese for ten vital days. In this photograph, a camouflaged Chinese infantryman runs to take up a new firing position in the Burmese jungle. (Keystone/ Getty Images)

The commander of the Chinese Fifth Army began deploying his troops in depth down the long Sittang valley in mid-March, as they slowly moved down the Burma Road by lorry and on foot to Lashio and onwards by train to Mandalay. The leading 8,500-strong motorized 200th Division, commanded by General Tai An-Lan, was tasked with defending the walled city of Toungoo, 60 miles to the south of the nearest other formation deployed at Pyinmana. The Japanese 55th Division advanced up the Sittang valley from Pegu on the night of 20/21 March, quickly encountering Chinese patrols that fought a series of delaying actions, and then a heavily fortified Chinese outpost position at Oktwin 12 miles south of Toungoo held by part of the Chinese 559th Regiment. Following fierce fighting, the Chinese battalion withdrew on 24 March having inflicted over 300 casualties on the Japanese spearhead. The Japanese 143rd Regiment swung westwards around the town on 24 March cutting it off from outside support to the west and overrunning the nearby airfield, while the 112th Regiment advanced astride the road towards Toungoo. The initial deliberate attack on the town by 55th Division on 25 March encountered stubborn resistance from the dug-in Chinese, who fought the Japanese to a standstill albeit at heavy cost. A series of direct infantry assaults on the old town, supported by heavy artillery and bombers and carried out by the increasingly exhausted 55th Division, failed to make ground, with determined Chinese Nationalist troops engaging in fierce house-to-house fighting and making repeated counter-attacks. Unfortunately, the orders given by Lieutenant-General Stilwell to the Chinese 22nd Division to attack in strength towards Toungoo from Yedashe were largely disobeyed, as were those issued to Sixth Army to send 55th Division from the Karen Hills in support. On 28 March, the newly deployed 56th Division's dismounted reconnaissance regiment crossed the Sittang River and swung around east of the town, nearly overrunning 200th Division's headquarters and threatening the formation's line of supply. The badly battered 200th Division now had little option but to withdraw from the burning town, which it did in good order on 29/30 April up the eastern bank of the river with its wounded, vehicles and heavy equipment. Unfortunately, in the confusion of the withdrawal, in the early hours of 30 March the Japanese seized intact the bridge over the Sittang River. The 200th Division had performed highly creditably during its stubborn protracted defence of Toungoo between 24 and 30 March, but the capture of the bridge over the Sittang by the enemy was a major disaster, with the Mawchi–Bawlake road it carried leading directly into the Karen Hills, the southern Shan States and then Lashio. The Japanese 18th and 55th divisions were now free to advance against the Chinese Fifth Army blocking the road and rail routes northwards to Mandalay. Meanwhile, the motorized 56th Division peeled off eastwards into the Shan States, exploiting a good network of roads leading towards Bawlake, Loikaw, Loilem and Lashio, and ultimately threatening to cut the Burma Road and the Chinese line of communications to Yunnan.

The Japanese 33rd Division pushed northwards up the Irrawaddy valley late in March towards Prome, a small town on the eastern bank of the Irrawaddy, with patrols making contact with Burcorps as they neared its outskirts. On 28 March, General Alexander ordered Burcorps to 'stage a demonstration' from Prome, to relieve pressure on the embattled Chinese at Toungoo. A column of Stuart light tanks, three battalions of lorried infantry and a field artillery battery, led by Brigadier John Anstice, quickly advanced southwards towards Padigon and the small town of Paungde, where limited resistance was met. A withdrawal was suddenly ordered, however, when news reached divisional headquarters that the road behind the motorized column had been blocked in the early hours of 29 March at Shwedaung by the Japanese II./215th Regiment (which had crossed from the western bank of the Irrawaddy). Two Indians battalions immediately attacked from the north to clear a roadblock at the Kala Chaung, but were halted by determined, dug-in enemy troops. A detachment of the BIA encountered north of Shwedaung fared less well, however, being dispersed with heavy losses by the IV./12th Frontier Force Regiment

The oilfields at Yenangyaung in central Burma provided Burcorps with its only source of petrol and engine oil following the fall of Rangoon. (Hulton-Deutsch Collection/Corbis via Getty Images)

A British soldier at left manning a 40mm Bofors gun enjoys a mug of hot tea as other troops look on. These light anti-aircraft guns provided a limited source of air defence to British troops following the destruction of Burwing on the ground. (Pen and Sword Books/ Universal Images Group via Getty Images)

late that afternoon. Repeated attacks from the south also failed to break through the resolute Japanese defenders of the roadblocks north and south of Shwedaung, and late on 30 March a desperate Anstice ordered his men to break out in small groups, leaving behind ten Stuarts, 200 soft-skin vehicles and two 25pdrs. Some 400 men were lost, and understandably morale plummeted. A flank guard of Royal Marines and commandos landed at Padaung on the western side of the river by Force Viper was successfully ambushed on 30 March by the Japanese III./215th Regiment and suffered heavy losses before withdrawing.

The Japanese 33rd Division attacked Prome on the evening of 1 April, although the British had already decided to withdraw 50 miles to cover the Yenangyaung oilfields, carrying out a series of delaying actions, conforming with the Chinese as they retired northwards from Toungoo. Japanese aircraft now ranged freely over Burma attacking Allied troops, road, rail and river communications and population centres. On 3 April, Mandalay was heavily bombed by the Japanese air force, causing heavy casualties as fire engulfed its wooden buildings. The 1st Burdiv – transported by train on 21 March from the Sittang valley to Taungdwingyi – deployed to the north of 17th Indian Division. The ground north of Prome, lying in the dry zone of central Burma, was very different from that in Tenasserim and the delta of the Irrawaddy River where British forces so far had fought, with the flat, undulating open terrain, broken only by patches of scrub, shallow stream beds and low bare hills, lending itself to the employment of motorized and tracked vehicles – albeit amidst clouds of dust that made them an easy mark to marauding Japanese aircraft. A combination of searing heat and acute shortages of drinking water during Burma's hottest month imposed considerable hardships upon already exhausted British, Indian, Gurkha and Burmese infantry and pack animals, who plodded northwards soaked in sweat amidst clouds of dust thrown up by vehicles. Sickness – malaria, dysentery and heat exhaustion – cut swathes through the ranks of already badly understrength units. The mood of many Burmese now increasingly swung against the withdrawing British, with apathy turning to sullen resentment and then open hostility. Indian and Anglo-Indian refugees escaping from local towns and villages proved an easy mark for merciless gangs of armed Burmese *dacoits* (bandits), who killed, raped and stole from these unfortunates seeking safety further north. Individual soldiers cut off from their units and small bands of stragglers also suffered attacks. Following defeat after defeat, understandably the numbers of Burma riflemen, whose homes and families vulnerable to attack were now far behind Japanese lines, deserting from 1st Burdiv rapidly increased.

Burcorps began occupying a new defensive line on 8 April, running from Minhla to Taungdwingyi, to meet the advancing 15,000-strong Japanese 33rd Division, which now deployed all three of its infantry regiments and received major support from an engineer regiment equipped with landing barges and launches. Under corps control, 2nd Burma Brigade held Minhla on the western side of the Irrawaddy River. The over-extended 1st Burdiv was deployed along a line anchored on the Irrawaddy River in the west that then ran 40 miles eastwards along a lateral road to the Taungdwingyi–Satthwa area that was defended by 17th Indian Division. The 33rd Division advanced on 9 April towards Yenangyaung, with its leading patrols making contact the following day with British positions between Alebo and Yagidaw. A diversionary Japanese assault by the Japanese 215th Regiment was rebuffed at Kokkogwa on the night of 11/12 April by the 48th Indian Infantry Brigade following fierce fighting, but the main Japanese effort near the river by the 213th Regiment forced 1st Burdiv to withdraw under heavy pressure on 14 April behind the Yin Chaung (a practically dry watercourse ten miles south of Magwe). The Japanese 214th Regiment infiltrated unnoticed into a wide gap that opened up between the 13th Indian Infantry Brigade and 48th Indian Infantry Brigade, crossed the lateral road and, still undiscovered, advanced to a new position 15 miles east of Magwe (40 miles south of Yenangyaung). On 15 April, it advanced again, eventually reaching

A group of lightly equipped Japanese infantryman pick their way through broken terrain during the heavy fighting near the Yenangyaung oilfields. The fighting nearly resulted in the complete destruction of 1st Burdiv. (Keystone/Getty Images)

a position 12 miles south-east of Yenangyaung and its vital oilfields, still undetected by its opponents. At 1300hrs that afternoon, Slim ordered the destruction of the oil wells, refineries and other key installations; this was completed by the end of the following day.

The Japanese 215th Regiment, meanwhile, maintained heavy pressure close to the riverbank. The 1st Burma Brigade, deployed on a line running behind the Yin Chaung, was heavily attacked at 0100hrs on 16 April, and the position only stabilized after a squadron of the 2nd Royal Tank Regiment intervened. The 1st Burdiv was forced to withdraw later that day in blistering 43-degree heat across a waterless area lying between the Yin Chaung and the abandoned oil town of Yenangyaung, where the next source of water was available. This physically punishing march continued the next day, imposing considerable hardship on the troops, harassed by low-flying Japanese aircraft, with leaping flames and clouds of 'apocalyptic' billowing black smoke marking the oilfields ahead in the distance. The Japanese 214th Regiment broke cover, and after

The city of Mandalay was largely destroyed after Japanese air raids caused fires that quickly spread through its wooden buildings unchecked. (© Imperial War Museum, K 2157)

quickly establishing strong roadblocks on the road north and south of the ford over the Pin Chaung (an unbridged river whose water level was low during the dry season) during the night of 16/17 April, seized Yenangyaung from the surprised garrison. A column of transport vehicles and escorting tanks sent back by Bruce Scott was briefly cut in half by the Japanese north of the river. The line of retreat of 1st Burdiv had been cut, with its exhausted, bedraggled and desperately thirsty officers and men nearing physical breakdown by the time they reached Yenangyaung (the worn-out rearguard arrived on the night of 17/18 April).

Following a hurried request for help from Lieutenant-General William Slim, the Chinese 38th Division, commanded by General Sun Li-Jen (part of the Sixty-Sixth Army that had just arrived at Mandalay), was put at Burcorps' disposal by Alexander and Stilwell the following day to extricate Burdiv from encirclement. The leading two regiments of the Chinese 38th Division, with British tanks and artillery under command, was tasked with clearing the Japanese roadblock north of the Pin Chaung at dawn on 18 April, while 13th Indian Infantry Brigade attacked the roadblock located at Twingon south of the river after advancing along a bypass road that skirted the eastern side of the town. The attack south of the Pin Chaung that began at 0630hrs on 18 April – despite the blazing sun, all-pervading stench of burning oil and an acute lack of water – was partially successful, with Magforce (an ad hoc force acting as the reserve for the 1st Burdiv that Slim had ordered across the Irrawaddy

The crew of an M3 Stuart light tank carry Chinese infantry into battle. The 38th Chinese Division was given powerful support by a squadron of M3 Stuart light tanks placed directly under its command during the Battle of Yenangyaung. (AirSeaLand)

THE BREAKOUT AT YENANGYAUNG, 1100HRS, 17 APRIL 1942 (PP. 68–69)

An M3A1 Stuart light tank (**1**) belonging to the 2nd Royal Tank Regiment (indicated by the green jeroboa/desert rat on front right fender, **2**) leads an Allied column northwards across the riverbed of the Pin Chaung during the final escape from encirclement during the battle of Yenangyaung. It is firing its 37mm coaxial machine gun (**3**). On the rear deck behind the turret are several wounded men (**4**). The vehicle is covered in the crew's kit and other odds and ends belonging to the crew.

Following the tank are several battle-worn soft-skin lorries (**5**), one marked as an ambulance with a Red Cross, another of which is in flames further to the rear. A column of British/Indian soldiers and pack animals (**6**) are plodding forward on foot – dirty, dusty and tired and in a few cases wounded, but with weapons at the ready.

In the background are wrecked oil derricks (**7**), buildings aflame and burning oil tanks scattered across the landscape. Plumes of black smoke are rising from demolitions of oil wells and other oil installations.

to Magwe) capturing Nyaunghla village after stiff fighting to protect the initial line of advance along the bypass. The I./18th Garwhalis and 1st Inniskillings (part of 13th Indian Infantry Brigade) advanced up the bypass, seized Hill 510 and then fought their way into Twingon, but were forcibly ejected by the Japanese after desperate hand-to-hand fighting. The Chinese attack north of the Pin Chaung was more successful and reached the riverbank east of the ford, but the Japanese still clung to a small bridgehead blocking the northern side of the crossing itself. Japanese pressure from the south against 1st Burdiv also

The oilfields of Yenangyaung – the scene of bitter fighting between Japanese troops and 1st Burma Division, which was virtually destroyed during frantic attempts to break out from enemy encirclement. (ullstein bild via Getty Images)

increased, with the 215th Regiment, dropped off by landing craft, moving into Yenangyaung and the 213th Regiment advancing from the east towards the town.

The fate of 1st Burdiv hung in the balance by mid-afternoon on 18 April, but a request made by a desperate Major-General Bruce Scott at 1630hrs for permission to break out over the Pin Chaung east of Twingon that night – abandoning his tanks, vehicles and seriously wounded – was calmly refused by the corps commander, who told him to hold on until a further coordinated Chinese attack from north of the river was organized the next day. Following a stressful but generally quiet night spent without water, harboured within a defensive perimeter astride the bypass, 13th Indian Infantry Brigade attacked the roadblock south of the ford at 0630hrs on 19 April, but once again met heavy resistance. The anxiously awaited Chinese attack at 0630hrs failed to appear, according to British accounts, and as the day dragged on – with heat exhaustion claiming an increasing toll of lives – Chinese troops were conspicuous by their absence. The 2nd King's Own Yorkshire Light Infantry (KOYLI) briefly crossed the Pin Chaung at midday, but an erroneous report that the Japanese had reached Gweygo to the north led to their withdrawal, and the opportunity was lost. A new crossing point was found by British tanks over the Pin Chaung, however, later that day 1½ miles east of Twingon, and with no signs of an imminent Chinese attack from the north, at 1400hrs Bruce Scott ordered a breakout by his exhausted and desperately thirsty men under Japanese mortar and gun fire down a rough track to the riverbank. The majority of wheeled vehicles, many carrying wounded or towing heavy equipment, bogged down in deep sand, with only tracked vehicles, mules and men staggering along on foot eventually crossing to the far bank. By nightfall the dispirited remnants of 1st Burdiv, having lost approximately 1,000 dead, wounded and missing, were safe several miles north of the Pin Chaung. Three hundred men entered Japanese captivity; many of the wounded abandoned at Yenangyaung were killed out of hand by the Japanese. The Chinese 38th Division's attack from the north, supported by British Stuart tanks, got under way at 1500hrs that afternoon. The leading Chinese troops, supported by the 2nd Royal Tank Regiment, crossed the river, rescuing British captives, and the next day seized a small hamlet west of Twingon, before briefly advancing into Yenangyaung itself. Having played a crucial part in allowing British troops to break contact, the following day it re-crossed the Pin Chaung and

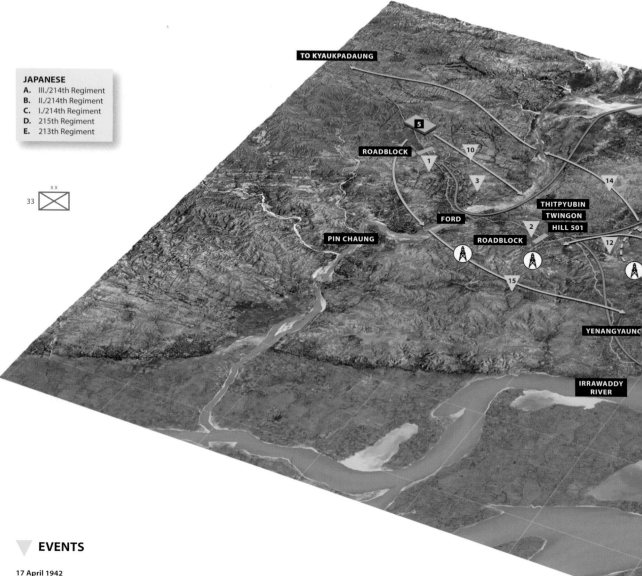

JAPANESE

A. III./214th Regiment
B. II./214th Regiment
C. I./214th Regiment
D. 215th Regiment
E. 213th Regiment

33

TO KYAUKPADAUNG

5

ROADBLOCK

10

1

3

14

THITPYUBIN

TWINGON

FORD

HILL 501

PIN CHAUNG

2

ROADBLOCK

12

15

YENANGYAUNG

IRRAWADDY
RIVER

▼ EVENTS

17 April 1942

1. The Japanese III./214th Regiment builds a roadblock north of the Pin Chaung.

2. The Japanese II./214th Regiment builds another roadblock to the south of the Pin Chaung ford, following which it occupies Twingon. 1st Burdiv's line of retreat is cut.

3. The Japanese roadblock north of the ford is cleared by British tanks and infantry, forcing the III./214th Regiment to withdraw to Twingon leaving behind a single company (9./III./214th) to hold a small bridgehead north of the Pin Chaung.

4. The I./214th Regiment travels upriver by boat and reinforces Japanese troops holding Yenangyaung.

5. 1st Burdiv moves northwards up the main road to Yenangyaung, already held in strength by the Japanese.

18 April 1942

6. 0630hrs: Magforce attacks up the road, clearing the Nyaunghla road far enough to prevent it coming under fire.

7. 13th Indian Infantry Brigade advances up the Nyaunghla Road and captures Hill 510, before moving northwards up the bypass to take Hill 501 and attack Twingon.

8. 1st Burdiv's transport follows 13th Indian Infantry Brigade up the bypass and along with 1st Burma Brigade concentrates at a road junction south of Twingon.

9. 1530hrs: Magforce withdraws and joins the rest of the division in a large perimeter camp set up near Twingon.

10. The Chinese 38th Division, supported by British tanks and artillery, attacks southwards and reaches the Pin Chaung, east of the ford.

11. Evening: The Japanese 215th Regiment travels upriver to Yenangyaung and reinforces the attack being made on 1st Burdiv, which is occupying the densely packed perimeter camp near Twingon.

19 April 1942

12. 0700hrs: 13th Indian Infantry Brigade attacks Twingon, but is repulsed with heavy casualties.

13. The Japanese 213th Regiment arrives and advances northwards towards the Pin Chaung.

14. 1400hrs: 1st Burdiv escapes from encirclement via a newly found shallow ford across the Pin Chaung 1½ miles east of Twingon, abandoning its wounded, vehicles and heavy equipment.

15. 1500hrs: The Chinese 38th Division attacks southwards and crosses the Pin Chaung. It briefly enters Yenangyaung, then withdraws on 20 April.

YENANGYAUNG, 17–19 APRIL 1942

Yenangyaung was another resounding victory for Japanese arms. Although the Japanese 33rd Division failed to capture the oilfields intact, Burcorps suffered a significant and sizeable defeat.

1 Burma

38 Chinese

TO MAGWE

HILL 510

NYAUNGHLA

SADAING

ALLIED
1. 1st Burma Division
2. Magforce
3. 13th Indian Infantry Brigade
4. 1st Burma Division's transport
5. Chinese 38th Division (reinforced)

Note: gridlines are shown at intervals of 2km (1.2 miles)

A three-man Indian crew fire a Mk I 3in. mortar. This simple weapon provided infantry battalions with a fast and highly flexible source of fire support, and could engage targets with high-explosive rounds up to 1,600 yards away. It could also fire smoke and illumination rounds. (AirSeaLand)

acted as rearguard while the remnants of Burdiv – destroyed as a fighting formation until it could reorganize – escaped northwards. It was another resounding victory for Japanese arms, although 33rd Division failed to capture the oilfields intact.

The Chinese Fifth Army blocking the Sittang valley also came under heavy Japanese pressure in mid/late April 1942 while fighting raged at Yenangyaung, with the Japanese 55th Division now reinforced by the 18th Division and the 1st Tank Regiment. A planned counter-offensive by Chinese troops south from Pyinmana proved stillborn after Burcorps' defeat at Yenangyaung and the collapse of Chinese resistance in the Shan States, with the hard-pressed 96th and 20th divisions withdrawing back towards Mandalay in considerable disorder. The Japanese 55th Division entered Pyinmana on 19 April, following which the fresh 18th Division took over the advance; on 20–21 April, the latter encountered two strong Chinese defensive positions north of the town that were only overcome after fierce fighting. The Japanese advance quickly gained momentum, with Pyabwe falling four days later into the hands of the 1st Tank Regiment unopposed, and soon after this motorized units from both divisions threatened the rail and road hub of Meiktila. The advancing Japanese now directly threatened Burcorps' line of communication through nearby Meiktila to Mandalay, as well as the vital supplies of food, ammunition and other stores stockpiled in the area. The Chinese left flank, meanwhile, had been turned, effectively ending any Allied hope of holding Burma, making it only a question of how long resistance could continue. The

A convoy of Red Cross vehicles in Burma, 8 April 1942. Hospital and medical supplies intended for China had to use the long and dangerous Burma Road, but the Japanese advance early in 1942 closed this route. Japanese Red Cross relief units were also despatched to Burma. (Keystone-France\Gamma-Rapho via Getty Images)

Japanese motorized 56th Division, supported by the 14th Tank Regiment, rampaged through the Shan States overwhelming the Chinese Temporary 55th Division, capturing Loikaw on 19 April and Loilem on 23 April and forcing back the crumbling and increasingly disorganized Chinese Sixth Army towards the Salween and Thai frontier. A counter-attack by 200th Division (sent eastwards by Stilwell to protect the flank of Fifth Army and Burcorps) began well by recapturing Taungyii on 24 April and then Loilem, but without warning this elite formation suddenly departed for Yunnan. On 29 April, Lashio fell into the hands of the Japanese 148th Regiment, cutting the Burma Road, and the regiment captured large stocks of petrol, arms, ammunition and vehicles destined for China. The Chinese Sixth Army had been dispersed in just two weeks. Fortunately for the Nationalist Chinese, on 24 April Lieutenant-General Iida had ordered Fifteenth Army to halt on the line of the Salween River instead of continuing virtually unopposed into Yunnan.

THE FINAL ALLIED WITHDRAWAL FROM BURMA

General Sir Harold Alexander, CO Burma Army between March and May 1942. By late April 1942, it was clear to Alexander that any further defence of northern Burma was impossible. (Bettman via Getty Images)

The Japanese victory over 1st Burdiv at Yenangyaung, against the Chinese Fifth Army defending Mandalay in the Sittang valley, and the virtual collapse of Chinese resistance in the face of the Japanese 56th Division's rapid advance eastwards through the Shan States made General Sir Harold Alexander accept by late April that the further defence of northern Burma was impossible with his shattered formations. Little option now remained other than deciding whether to retreat to India or into China. Following deliberations with Wavell, Stilwell and the Chinese, on 28 April Alexander ordered Slim to retreat to India, with a withdrawal via the Chindwin valley and up the Kalewa–Tamu route across the mountains quickly emerging as the only practicable option for British arms, while the remnants of the CEF either retreated northwards or eastwards towards Yunnan. Work immediately began stocking the route and evacuating as many administrative troops, families and refugees as possible ahead of the fighting troops. The fast-approaching monsoon (expected to break with full fury about 20 May) and dwindling stores added impetus to the decision by General Alexander to escape to north-eastern India.

Burcorps briefly covered the Chinese Fifth Army's withdrawal to Mandalay with 7th Armoured Brigade, before it withdrew on 25–26 April from Meiktila. A brief delaying action was fought by the 2nd Royal Tank Regiment against the Japanese II./114th Regiment, supported by tanks, north of the town the following day. This bought 48th Indian Infantry Brigade – the most combat-capable formation in Burcorps – sufficient time to dig in at Kyaukse (30 miles south of

Japanese troops led by an officer brandishing a sword advance through clouds of smoke and dust towards the city of Mandalay. (adoc-photos/Corbis via Getty Images)

Mandalay), where it was tasked with holding up two enemy divisions and a tank regiment until 1800hrs on 29 April. The I./7th Gurkha Rifles clashed with Japanese motorized troops late on 28 April south of the Kykause, and a series of Japanese unsuccessful attacks by elements of 18th Division were made overnight on the main defensive positions. The Gurkhas, closely supported by Stuart tanks, counter-attacked the following morning, before 48th Indian Infantry Brigade broke contact as planned at 1800hrs that evening from its pursuers. It had been a virtually textbook example of a successful rearguard action that checked the advance of a superior enemy force. The 63rd Indian Infantry Brigade was the last formation to cross the ¾-mile-long Ava Bridge (the only one over the Irrawaddy); at 2320hrs on 30 April, it was rendered impassable by the demolition of two of its spans. The 1st Burdiv, meanwhile, crossed further west at Sameikkon by ferry and moved westwards at a pace determined by its plodding bullock-cart transport towards Monywa.

The still-jubilant Japanese Fifteenth Army had failed in its immediate objective of destroying either Burcorps or the Chinese Fifth Army south of the Irrawaddy, but the way was now open to conquer northern Burma and potentially encircle and destroy the remaining Allied forces by

A group of Japanese infantrymen, part of 18th Division, dash through the burnt-out ruins of the city of Mandalay. (ullstein bild via Getty Images)

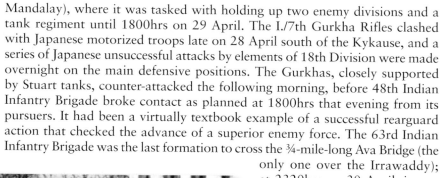

another lightning advance. The Japanese 33rd Division quickly moved towards Monywa, a small town nestling on the Chindwin's eastern bank 50 miles north of the confluence of the Chindwin and Irrawaddy, hoping to block Burcorps' escape. The Japanese 55th Division pushed northwards towards Myitkyina, with one regiment striking up the railway line towards Shwebo and another up the eastern bank of the Irrawaddy to Katha, while other detached units captured Maymyo and Mogok. On 1 May, the Japanese 18th Division occupied the still-smouldering city of Mandalay without opposition, after which it mopped up the last remaining Chinese forces holding out in the Shan States. The motorized 56th Division continued to move rapidly eastwards, meanwhile, fully exploiting its mobility to keep the disintegrating Chinese Sixth Army on the run. Following the capture of Lashio on 29 April, a single regiment proceeded towards the bridge over the Salween River inside China, while others moved northwards towards Bhamo. It fell to the Japanese 56th Reconnaissance Regiment on 3 May, and then Myitkyina was captured by the Japanese 146th Regiment on 8 May. Little resistance was encountered from the increasingly demoralized Chinese Fifth and Sixth armies. Further north the Chinese HQ Fifth Army and 22nd Division, now cut off by the Japanese capture of Myitkyina, withdrew westwards towards Maingkawan in the malaria-ridden Hukawng valley accompanied by an estimated 10,000 refugees, en route eventually to Assam in India, while the rest of the disorganized CEF retreated north and then eastwards towards its homeland.

Sick and wounded Chinese soldiers receive medical treatment. The Chinese Expeditionary Force had few medical units and relied heavily for assistance upon the British and a volunteer unit organized and run by Dr Gordon Seagrave – a US missionary resident in Burma. (Pen and Sword Books/Universal Images Group via Getty Images)

Burcorps deployed along a line north of the Irrawaddy River after the Ava Bridge was demolished, with only 6,500 British, 22,000 Indian and 4,000 Burmese combatant troops now fit to fight. The Chindwin valley, and then across the high mountains from Tamu into north-eastern India, was chosen by General Alexander as the main route for Burma Army's escape when it became clear a further defence of northern Burma was impracticable; the exception was 2nd Burma Brigade, which left Pakkoku on 28 April to withdraw up the Myittha valley to Kalemyo. A handful of transport aircraft continued to evacuate wounded and refugees from airfields at Myitkyina and Shwebo, meanwhile, until attacks by Japanese fighters forced its abandonment. The fighting spirit of Burcorps remained surprisingly high, but as it moved westwards towards Monywa, morale collapsed in many administrative units (which had performed creditably to date transferring food, ammunition and stores from Rangoon to Mandalay and in keeping the army supplied in the field), and mobs of ill-disciplined troops seeking safety preceded it westwards.

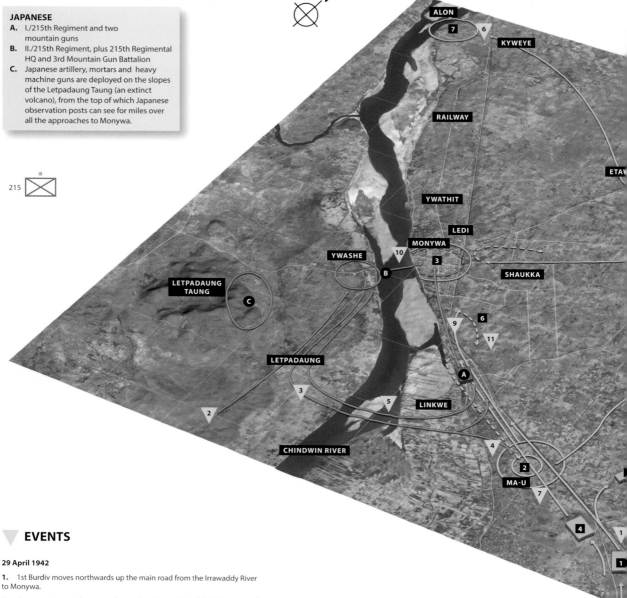

JAPANESE

A. I./215th Regiment and two mountain guns

B. II./215th Regiment, plus 215th Regimental HQ and 3rd Mountain Gun Battalion

C. Japanese artillery, mortars and heavy machine guns are deployed on the slopes of the Letpadaung Taung (an extinct volcano), from the top of which Japanese observation posts can see for miles over all the approaches to Monywa.

215

ALON

KYWEYE

RAILWAY

ETA

YWATHIT

LEDI

MONYWA

YWASHE

SHAUKKA

LETPADAUNG TAUNG

LETPADAUNG

LINKWE

CHINDWIN RIVER

MA-U

▼ EVENTS

29 April 1942

1. 1st Burdiv moves northwards up the main road from the Irrawaddy River to Monywa.

2. Japanese troops advance up the western bank of the Chindwin and reach Ywashe at sunset opposite Monywa.

3. Japanese patrols cross the river from Letpadaung to Linkwe.

30 April 1942

4. 1st Burma Division's HQ is overrun at Ma-u by a Japanese patrol.

01 May 1942

5. The Japanese I./215th Regiment and two mountain guns cross the river at Letpadaung and at 0900hrs seize Monywa from the south. The newly occupied town is prepared for all-round defence.

6. At Alon, 2,400 Allied clerks and their families evacuated from AHQ await transport upriver by steamer.

7. The 63rd Indian Brigade detrains at Kyehmon, moves northwards and attacks Monywa astride the main road, but after overcoming strong resistance at Ma-u fails to enter Monywa. Overnight it occupies a perimeter camp at Ma-u.

02 May 1942

8. The 13th Indian Infantry Brigade moves cross-country to Zalok and attacks south-west astride the Monywa–Shwebo road, with the V./1st Punjabis briefly capturing the railway station.

9. The 63rd Indian Brigade attacks simultaneously up the railway from the south from the perimeter camp at Ma-u, but encounters fierce Japanese resistance.

10. The Japanese II./215th Regiment crosses the Chindwin from Ywashe and is reinforced later in the day by 215th Regimental HQ and 3rd Mountain Gun Battalion.

11. The weak 1st Burma Brigade is committed to battle at 1500hrs from reserve, but after passing through 63rd Indian Infantry Brigade, its successful attack is called off an hour later.

12. 1st Burma Division's transport and then fighting troops disengage and swing cross-country around Monywa to Alon, where it is joined by headquarters 7th Armoured Brigade, before proceeding northwards to Ye-u.

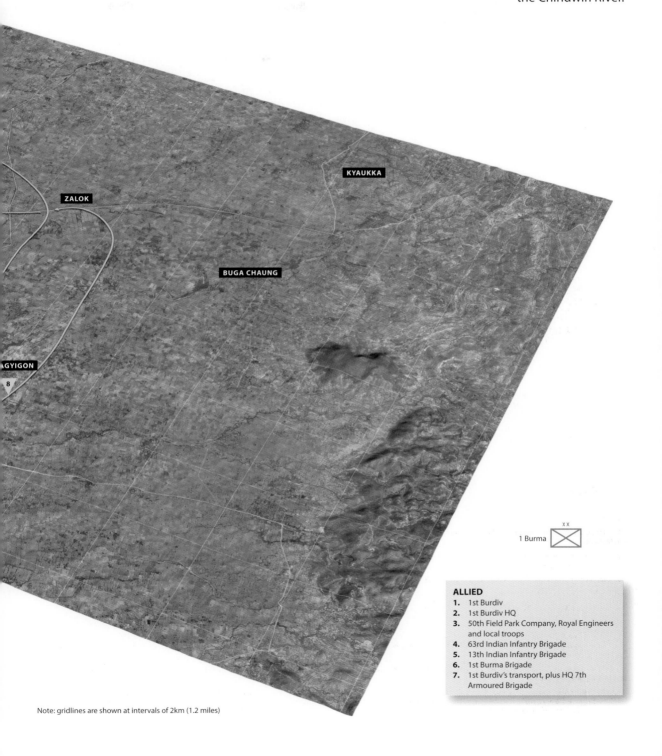

MONYWA, 30 APRIL–1 MAY 1942

The loss of Monywa was a devastating blow, effectively outflanking the British defences on the Irrawaddy, threatening 1st Burdiv's escape and disrupting Burma Army's planned withdrawal route to India using the Shwegyin–Kalewa crossing over the Chindwin River.

KYAUKKA

ZALOK

BUGA CHAUNG

GYIGON

8

1 Burma   X X

ALLIED
1. 1st Burdiv
2. 1st Burdiv HQ
3. 50th Field Park Company, Royal Engineers and local troops
4. 63rd Indian Infantry Brigade
5. 13th Indian Infantry Brigade
6. 1st Burma Brigade
7. 1st Burdiv's transport, plus HQ 7th Armoured Brigade

Note: gridlines are shown at intervals of 2km (1.2 miles)

The Japanese 33rd Division nearly intercepted Burcorps before it escaped. On 29 April, the Japanese I./215th Regiment crossed the Chindwin River and occupied Pakokku, exploiting a gap Slim inadvertently left in British dispositions by 2nd Burma Brigade's departure up the Myittha valley (this formation was not pursued by enemy troops as it withdrew northwards). It was then transported 45 miles northwards aboard lorries up a rough track running along the western bank of the river to a point opposite Monywa, from where mortars and artillery – directed from an obervation post atop an extinct volcano – brought this small riverside town under fire. Under cover of darkness, Japanese patrols quickly crossed the 600-yard-wide river that night, and discovered British troops were thin on the ground. A surprise attack by a small Japanese raiding party in the early hours of 30 April overran 1st Burdiv's headquarters at Ma-u. This shocking news and the sound of shellfire in the distance persuaded Burcorps headquarters, 16 miles away at Songon, to hurriedly decamp to Ye-u. The largely undefended town of Monywa fell into Japanese hands at 0900hrs on 1 May after the Japanese I./215th Regiment and two regimental guns crossed the river in three launches and attacked from the south. The loss of Monywa was a devastating blow, effectively outflanking the British defences on the Irrawaddy, threatening 1st Burdiv's escape and disrupting Burma Army's planned withdrawal route to India using the Shwegyin–Kalewa crossing over the Chindwin. The 1st Burma Brigade and 13th Indian Infantry Brigade were still 20 miles away, but both quickly marched northwards to the sound of the guns. A counterattack by 63rd Indian Infantry Brigade (rushed by railway from near the Ava Bridge) northwards from Kyehmon the next morning, supported by a squadron of the 7th Hussars, failed to dislodge the Japanese (now reinforced by the II./215th Regiment, regimental headquarters and later a mountain artillery battalion), with the town's defenders enjoying powerful artillery, mortar and machine gun support from across the river. The 63rd Indian

The M3 Stuart light tank – armed with a 37mm main gun and machine guns – equipped 7th Armoured Brigade's two regiments. The Stuart provided Burcorps with an invaluable source of mobile fire support during the pitched fighting in central Burma. (© Imperial War Museum, KF 286)

Infantry Brigade attacked again at 0840hrs the following morning from Ma-u, with the newly arrived 13th Indian Infantry Brigade also attacking Monywa from the east from Zalok, but both assaults made across flat, open paddy ground to a halt at the outskirts despite strong artillery support. The 1st Burma Infantry Brigade, committed from reserve at 1545hrs, made some progress, but its attack was called off when an order was received (whose origins have been disputed) to abandon all efforts to recapture Monywa, skirt the town and pull back to Alon. The 1st Burdiv bypassed the town overnight, and the rest marched or were ferried by lorry northwards to Ye-u, where it was joined on 3/4 May by the rest of 17th Indian Division and the main body of 7th Armoured Brigade who had travelled via a track from Shwebo following the abandonment of the Mandalay–Irrawaddy line. The 16th Indian Infantry Brigade was immediately sent ahead by lorry to secure the small village of Shwegyin, from where river steamers ran a ferry service six miles upstream to Kalewa on the western bank of the Chindwin River. To escape, speed was now of the essence, with stocks of food dwindling (on 4 May Burma Army was put on half-rations), the Japanese threatening the crossing at Shwegyin–Kalewa and with the predicted date of the monsoon's arrival on 20 May fast approaching.

The loss of Monywa, giving the Japanese free passage upriver towards Kalewa by boat and denying the lower Chindwin to British river traffic, meant practically the whole of Burma Army now had to quickly retire westwards up the 107-mile-long Ye-u–Shwegyin track. This difficult route, snaking backwards and forwards through dense jungle, required major improvement by hard-pressed sappers, who had to hurriedly build bamboo bridges, straighten hairpin bends and lay corduroy trackways made from tree trunks over the sandy beds of dry *chaungs* (streams) to enable wheeled vehicles to pass. Supply dumps, water points and a traffic control system on the clogged track were hurriedly established for both troops and thousands of exhausted Indian, Anglo-Indian and Anglo-Burmese refugees slogging towards safety. The much-depleted 1st Burdiv led the way from Kaduma onwards, accompanied by over 2,300 sick and wounded, with 13th Indian Infantry Brigade reaching Shwegyin on 7 May. A single understrength battalion was left to guard the village, while the main body quickly proceeded upriver to defend Kalewa and Sittaung from surprise attack. The 1st Burma Infantry Brigade moved independently cross-country northwards on foot up the eastern bank of the Chindwin River via Indaw, providing a flank guard, before crossing over the river at Pantha en route to Tamu. To protect Shwegyin against a Japanese advance upriver by boat, a sampan boom was put in place 1½ miles south of the village at Gaundi, with a small Royal Marine detachment and Indian troops guarding each end. Several air raids by RAF Blenheims from No. 113 Squadron operating from Bengal, moreover, were made on enemy river traffic near Monywa to disrupt any move upriver. A jetty was quickly built in a sandy bay where the Shwegyin *chaung* entered the Chindwin River, and the slow and laborious process of getting the sick, wounded and administrative troops, as well as thousands of refugees, across the Chindwin using six sternwheel paddle steamers – each carrying 600–700 passengers and four vehicles – immediately began. Further delay was caused by a series of intermittent Japanese air attacks, following which the reluctant Indian and Burmese crews refused to work in daylight hours. This small village proved the end of the road for nearly

Burmese children play atop a burnt-out wreck of a Stuart light tank. The Imperial Japanese Army salvaged several of the vehicles lost by 7th Armoured Brigade during the Retreat from Burma and pressed them into service. (Keystone-France\Gamma-Rapho via Getty Images)

all of Burcorps' wheeled and tracked vehicles, parked closely together along with derelict civilian cars on a half-mile-long and 400-yard-wide area of open paddy field surrounded by a 200ft-high steep escarpment (dubbed 'the Basin'), due to a lack of deck space on each steamer and loading facilities. These included 7th Armoured Brigade's last few remaining Stuarts, which were wrecked by their crews to deny them to the enemy. The majority of army- and corps-level units had crossed to Kalewa upstream on the western bank by the time the headquarters of 17th Indian Division arrived on 8 May. The headquarters and remainder of 1st Burdiv crossed the river on the night of 8/9 May, followed the next day by the 63rd Indian Infantry Brigade and the 2nd Royal Tank Regiment.

The 48th Indian Infantry Brigade stayed behind at Pyingaing (dubbed 'Pink Gin' by British soldiers) for four days, buying vital time for the fighting troops, non-combatant units and refugees moving ahead on the Ye-u track to reach and cross the Chindwin. It departed on the night of 8/9 May, and after being picked up by lorries reached Shwegyin and harboured just outside the Basin at Mutaik late that evening. A large part of Burcorps had already departed by the time 48th Indian Infantry Brigade arrived, but the headquarters of 17th Indian Divison, assorted troops and refugees still awaited their turn, queuing near the jetty. The Japanese – bold, tenacious and highly aggressive to the last – had not abandoned hope of destroying Burcorps once and for all. On the evening of 4 May, Araki Force (33rd Division's headquarters, 213th Infantry Regiment and a mountain artillery battalion) moved northwards under Lieutenant-General Sakurai's personal command from Monywa, with some travelling upriver aboard

The Battle at Shwegyin, 9–11 May 1942

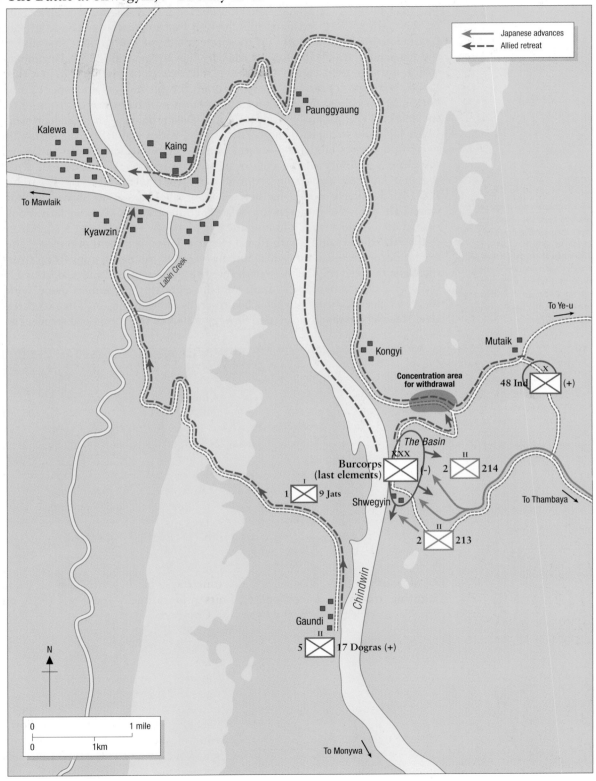

Japanese advances

Allied retreat

Paunggyaung

Kalewa

Kaing

To Mawlaik

Kyawzin

Labin Creek

Kongyi

To Ye-u

Mutaik

Concentration area
for withdrawal

48 Ind (+)

The Basin

Burcorps
(last elements)

2 214

1 9 Jats

Shwegyin

To Thambaya

2 213

N

Gaundi

5 17 Dogras (+)

Chindwin

0   1 mile
0   1km

To Monywa

motorboats and landing craft and the rest marching up the eastern bank. The river-borne force disembarked undetected nine miles south of Shwegyin on the night of 9/10 May and marched on foot northwards. The I./9th Jat Regiment, holding outposts on the eastern side of the Basin, came under sudden attack at 0545hrs on 10 May by the Japanese II./213th Regiment, which initially tried to advance down the *chaung* to the jetty. When this failed, Japanese troops infiltrated through the Jat piquets and opened fire with machine guns, mortars and a mountain gun from the clifftops onto the packed troops and refugees in the Basin below. The hard-pressed I./9th Jats held firm, with the I./7th Gurkha Rifles stabilizing the situation by 0900hrs after launching several fierce counter-attacks. Unfortunately, the close proximity of the enemy meant the jetty was abandoned, with the last steamer departing from it early that morning. The Japanese II./214th Regiment added further weight to the assault on Shwegyin, but were halted by the intervention of two understrength Gurkha battalions rushed up to hold a track running north from the Basin to Kaing. A squadron of the 7th Hussars and II./5th Royal Gurkha Rifles were held in reserve. The 40mm Bofors anti-aircraft guns, 3in. mortars and mountain guns firing from the Basin deluged the Japanese with shellfire. A battery of 25pdrs, part of 1st Indian Field Regiment, at Mutaik added weight to the bombardment, with its crews gleefully using up their last reserves of ammunition. The last three river steamers to reach embattled Shwegyin picked up troops and refugees at

A long column of Japanese infantry marches along a track through the Burmese jungle in early May 1942. The initial and final phases of the Retreat from Burma took place in dense tropical and semi-tropical jungle. (Keystone-France\Gamma-Rapho via Getty Images)

about 1400hrs from a new landing place sheltered by steep cliffs 200 yards upriver. At 2015hrs, after darkness had fallen, the 48th Indian Infantry Brigade broke contact and withdrew – after setting ablaze the remaining vehicles, artillery, ammunition, stores and equipment abandoned at Shwegyin – along precipitous, narrow jungle paths up the eastern riverbank to Kaing, to a point opposite Kalewa from where its men crossed the river to safety the following day. Fortunately for the Allies, the victorious Japanese contented themselves with collecting prisoners and salvaging arms, ammunition and equipment from the wreck of Burma Army's defeat.

The rearguard of Burcorps – 63rd Indian Infantry Brigade – did not hang about at Kalewa, given the fast-approaching monsoon and the appalling state of the route up the Kabaw valley to Manipur lying ahead. On the morning of 12 May, it left, with some marching afoot and the rest travelling upriver to Sittaung, where the river steamers were scuttled. The first heavy rains of the monsoon broke that day, although fortunately for the Allies the weather stayed fair for the remainder of the week as the ragged survivors of Burcorps trudged westwards towards safety. The initial stage of the withdrawal to Tamu (a small village just inside the Indian frontier lying at a height of 500ft above sea level) took place along a recently improved road suitable for wheeled traffic in the dry season that had been stocked with rations. It then turned into a narrow and increasingly steep, winding and muddy track, crossing innumerable streams that threatened to turn into raging torrents if heavy rain began, running through thick highly malarial jungle, to Palel at the southern edge of the Imphal Plain. En route it crossed over the 5,000ft-high Shenam Saddle, before descending onto the Imphal Plain below to the west, where motor transport awaited. It was a race against time before the full fury of the monsoon broke and transformed the track into an impassable quagmire. This long and difficult jungle track proved a harsh ordeal for the gaunt, ragged, sick and exhausted officers and men of Burcorps – some of whom were wounded – slogging through the jungle, accompanied by long lines of emaciated Indian refugees, most suffering badly from malnutrition and desperately ill from malaria, typhus and other tropical diseases endemic in the border areas. Many who had travelled to India well in advance of the fighting troops (30,000 passed that way in March and another 30,000 in April) had succumbed en route, with rotting bodies littering the track and nearby jungle further adding to the horror of the withdrawal. Whenever possible the 50 remaining four-wheel-drive lorries and jeeps – whose main role was carrying the wounded – ferried troops forward. On 18 May, the full fury of the monsoon rains was unleashed, but the final troops of Burcorps were within reach of their final destination, aided in part by an Indian Motor Transport Company sent down from Imphal to south of Tamu to assist by ferrying troops. On 21 May, 48th Indian Infantry Brigade passed through 23rd Indian Division (part of Lieutenant-General Noel Irwin's newly deployed IV Corps) holding the Shenam Saddle and arrived at Palel, where it was joined the following day by 63rd Indian Infantry Brigade bringing up the rear. Some 30,000 men from Burma Army had reached safety along with ten 25pdrs, 14 3.7in. mountain guns and four 2pdr anti-tank guns, 30 jeeps, 50 four-wheel-drive lorries and a single one of 7th Armoured Brigade's prized Stuart tanks (named *The Curse of Scotland*). On 20 May 1942, IV Corp assumed operational command of all troops in Burma Army, which formally ceased to exist.

The 3½-month-long 'Retreat from Burma' was over.

ASSESSMENT

The Burma Army had successfully completed a lengthy fighting retreat covering over 1,000 miles – the longest withdrawal ever carried out by British arms – northwards from Rangoon through central Burma, over wide, fast-flowing rivers and then by rough tracks over the high jungle-covered mountains towards India. It was an amazing achievement, carried out mostly in contact with the enemy, especially since it had transported its own administrative base with it for the last 700 miles during some of the hottest and driest weather experienced each year in Burma. The arrival of the sick, exhausted and badly battered Burcorps at Imphal was quite justifiably a source of huge pride for Lieutenant-General William Slim and his small staff, with his command having survived as a 'force in being', and still capable of fighting. Most of Burcorps' men would recover to fight again, but a good number were left permanently incapacitated by tropical disease and injuries sustained during this short-lived campaign. The Retreat from Burma made Lieutenant-General Slim's name, who emerged from it as a hero in the minds of Burcorps' men, inspired by his charismatic personality, no-nonsense style of leadership and dogged determination to keep fighting. It must not be forgotten, however, that Burcorps had been preceded by a large disorganized 'mob' of ill-disciplined administrative troops, whose units had disintegrated following the withdrawal across the Irrawaddy River. A total of 30,000 officers and men from Burma Army reached India – 12,000–13,000 fighting troops in Burcorps – with the majority serving in assorted army, corps and miscellaneous administrative and support units. A heavy price was paid in lives, reputations and imperial prestige by the British military authorities in Burma for seriously underestimating the Japanese, lack of preparedness and on occasion sheer incompetence: 1,499 dead, 2,595 wounded and 9,369 reported missing were suffered by British, Indian and Gurkha units in total during the entire campaign. The Japanese later reported a total of 4,918 prisoners of war.

Japanese soldiers carefully search a captured British soldier for concealed weapons and information. A harsh fate awaited Commonwealth troops in Japanese prisoner of war camps, with many labouring on back-breaking construction projects. (AirSeaLand)

The Chinese Expeditionary Force had not fared so well during the last stages of the campaign. It had played a key role fighting the Japanese in 1942, and without the CEF's support it is highly likely the badly outnumbered Burma Army would have been destroyed in detail or forced to surrender. Following the stubborn week-long resistance offered by the Chinese 200th Division to the Japanese at Toungoo, the CEF had faced the greater part of Fifteenth Army – holding up two Japanese divisions in the Sittang valley and engaging another in the Shan States – mostly unaided. It had also played a significant part in the fighting in the Irrawaddy valley, with the 38th Division rescuing 1st Burdiv from encirclement at Yenangyaung. Overall, the CEF lost heavily in Burma in 1942 – suffering approximately 25,000 casualties – with Fifth and Sixth armies losing two-thirds of their original strength and the Sixty-Sixth Army losing approximately one-third, as discipline and morale broke down during its pell-mell retreat to Yunnan. The highly regarded Chinese 38th Division made good its escape to India, arriving late in May, as did the headquarters of Fifth Army and remnants of the 22nd Division later in July via the Hukawng valley, but also at heavy cost from enemy action and tropical disease.

A final accounting cannot ignore the plight of the unfortunate Burmese population during the Japanese invasion in 1942. It had suffered heavily under indiscriminate Japanese air attacks on towns scattered across the country and from the fighting that had raged across southern, central and northern Burma that left behind a legacy of death, destruction and chaos.

Following the disintegration of the Chinese Expeditionary Force in central and northern Burma, US General Joseph 'Vinegar Joe' Stilwell and his staff escaped (after abandoning their vehicles) on foot along jungle paths to India. (MPI/ Getty Images)

The failure of their European colonial masters – whose prestige plummeted – to protect the colony against an attack by an Asian power had clear political implications, with the discontented, disillusioned and desperate population a fertile breeding ground for Aung San and Burmese nationalists, who had secured de facto political independence from the UK albeit under the close control of another colonial master. The political genie was out of the bottle, and the cork would never be replaced. The fate of the refugees during the disastrous evacuation of Burma must not be forgotten either in the final accounting. Fear of the Japanese and Burmese retribution had caused swarms of Europeans, Indians, Anglo-Indians and Anglo-Burmese refugees – 366,000 according to a recent study – to make their way out of Burma. The exact number of refugees, whose bodies littered the escape routes to India, will never be known, but recent research estimates 80,000 men, women and children may have died from enemy action and exhaustion, cholera, tropical disease and malnutrition.

The escape of Burma Army to India should not hide the unpalatable truth that British arms had been trounced by a highly professional, aggressive and resourceful Japanese opponent, whose leaders had displayed superior generalship and whose troops had repeatedly outfought British Commonwealth and Nationalist Chinese soldiers on the battlefield. The Japanese Fifteenth Army had achieved a stunning victory in Burma, coming close on the heels of the surrender of Malaya Command on Singapore Island, at minimal cost – 4,597 killed and wounded. Following just 5½ months of bitter fighting Imperial Japan had bundled the British out of Burma and achieved all its objectives: the vital oilfields in the conquered Netherland East Indies were now out of range of Allied air

Stilwell and personnel from the Chinese Fifth and Sixth armies and Allied staff make their way along the Uyu River in Burma during their retreat into India in mid-1942. (US Army)

power; it had cut the Burma Road to China; it had access to Burmese rice, timber, wolfram and oil; and there was the added bonus that its troops now directly threatened the security of eastern India (the loss of Burmese rice was a contributory factor in the disastrous Bengal famine in 1943) – although the largely impenetrable mountains and monsoon had brought the Japanese onrush to a halt. The vast majority of Imperial Japanese Army formations deployed in Burma had fought hard and extremely well, with the Japanese 33rd Division (according to Louis Allan), for example, having taken part in 34 engagements, marched 127 days and covered over 1,500 miles at the rate of 30 miles a day. The ordinary Japanese soldier emerged from the fighting in Burma in 1942 with an ill-deserved reputation in the minds of their opponents as an unbeatable 'superman' and quite erroneously as being a highly trained jungle fighter. The Japanese Fifteenth Army came within a hair's breadth of destroying Burma Army in detail on two occasions: at the Taukkyan roadblock on 7–8 March and latterly at Monywa on 30 May–1 April. It was only by a stroke of pure luck that the Rangoon garrison, 17th Indian Division and 7th Armoured Brigade, escaped destruction at Taukkyan when the Japanese withdrew. Similarly, it was also a very close-run thing that 1st Burdiv escaped being destroyed at Yenangyaung in April, albeit at the cost of most of its vehicles, heavy weapons and other equipment.

The Burma Army had been given a task well beyond its powers in holding back the Imperial Japanese Army, whose invasion succeeded so quickly because of long-term British failure to put in place adequate defensive arrangements to protect the colony from foreign aggression. The bitter seeds of defeat in Burma had been sown and taken root long, long before January 1942, dating back to the decision to base the strategic defence of the entire Far East on the Singapore Naval Base and the assumption that internal security would be the only role of Burma

Army. Senior officers at New Delhi never perceived a credible external threat to pre-war Burma from Imperial Japan due to distance, geography and the Royal Navy, nor did those in London after April 1937. This meant very little progress was made in constructing strategic roads and a rail infrastructure linking India and Burma, or in building up the requisite armed forces, facilities and stockpiles within the colony. Surprisingly perhaps, little changed even after the Second Sino-Japanese War broke out in 1937 and the beginning of World War II in Europe in September 1939, with the colony coming very low down the list of priorities for the very limited supplies of arms, ammunition and men sent from Europe to the Far East, certainly compared to Malaya Command – still regarded as the bulwark of Far Eastern defence.

The fate of Burma in 1942 was ultimately decided on the battlefield in Tenasserim and southern Burma, when ironically perhaps the Japanese Fifteenth Army was at its weakest, fielding only two understrength divisions dependent on pack animals for transport and supply and with very limited mountain artillery support. The Burma Army was outfought from the outset, suffering repeated defeats on the battlefield at Japanese hands, who owed their success to aggressive light infantry tactics carried out by its highly trained, well-organized and lightly equipped troops. The latter ruthlessly exploited the cover and concealment provided by the jungle to full effect to outflank, bypass and encircle their bewildered enemy, rather than having any specialized jungle training. The harsh truth is that the young, inexperienced, poorly trained and badly equipped Burmese units and British, Indian and Gurkha troops sent from India Command who opposed the Japanese were sent like lambs to the slaughter in the Burmese jungle. The rapid expansion of the Burma Rifles and Burma Frontier Force since 1940 from a tiny base had done little to improve their efficiency, with arms and equipment in short supply and too few experienced officers and NCOs available to carry out urgent remedial training. These units fought poorly, and understandably desertion was rife from poorly trained new Burmese units, who suffered repeated defeats and whose families were quickly left behind in enemy-controlled areas subjected to enemy intimidation. The overall fighting effectiveness of the Indian Army reinforcements had been deplorably low, largely as a result of decisions made thousands of miles away in London to expand it at too hurried a rate and organize, equip and train it for warfare in the Middle East. The root cause of the defeat of British, Indian, Gurkha and Burmese troops was not a failure to organize, equip and train for jungle fighting (as some have claimed), but rather lay in pitting young, raw and inexperienced troops of just three months' service with inadequate basic training in battle against mostly hardened professionals. While some further basic instruction was given and men were introduced to the jungle, it was not enough. The long 'tails' of tracked and wheeled first-line transport and heavy equipment accompanying fighting units, originally intended to fight in the wide-open spaces of the Middle East, tied them to the roads, making them vulnerable to lightly equipped Japanese troops who encircled them again and again. Understandably, the morale of such units proved brittle and plummeted as the campaign progressed from a very low starting point, following repeated defeats and under constant attacks from the air; some units from the Indian Army,

Burma Rifles and Burma Frontier Force disintegrated.

Not all British Commonwealth units, however, can be tarred with the same brush. The magnificent courage and reliance displayed by the VII./10th Baluch Regiment at Kuzeik (even though a defeat) showed just what even war-raised Indian Army battalions were capable of in a pitched battle with the Imperial Japanese Army. The spirited resistance offered by the 48th Indian Infantry Brigade at Kokkogwa on 11–14 April, containing a high proportion of well-trained Gurkhas, was regarded by the Japanese 33rd Division as its first real defeat of the campaign. On 28 April, the same formation administered a sharp drubbing to the advancing Japanese 18th Division at Kyaukse. The battle-hardened and highly experienced British 7th Armoured Brigade, operating in terrain where the firepower and mobility of its Stuart light tanks could be fully exploited, formed the linchpin of Burcorps' defence in central Burma, playing a vital role in shoring up the crumbling will and ability to resist of other units.

A group of Japanese soldiers look on in awe in March 1942 at the greatly revered 66m-long statue of the Reclining Buddha at Chaukhtatgyi Temple in Rangoon. (CPA Media Pte Ltd/Alamy)

The end of the Retreat from Burma in May 1942 amidst the teeming monsoon rains on the Imphal Plain marked just the beginning of the single longest campaign of World War II, ending with Fourteenth Army, led by General Sir William Slim, back in Mandalay and Rangoon and a comprehensively beaten Imperial Japanese Army only just hanging on to that part of Burma lying east of the Sittang River. The survivors of Burcorps who reached Imphal brought back to India a treasure trove of lessons and practical experience about living, moving and fighting in the jungle against Imperial Japanese troops that laid the foundations for future success. The many lessons learnt in Burma in 1941–42, combined with those gathered by the Australian Imperial Force in New Guinea, would form the basis of the revolution in jungle fighting doctrine, tactics and training carried out in India Command following the Retreat from Burma and disastrous First Arakan Campaign between 1943 and 1945. Three long years of hard fighting lay ahead before the revitalized 'new' Indian Army fought its way back over the border mountains and across Burma. This was only made possible by the Japanese Fifteenth Army's own calamitous defeat at the Battle of Imphal-Kohima between March and July 1944, which paved the way for an advance across the mountains, over the rivers Chindwin and Irrawaddy and back into central Burma.

THE BATTLEFIELD TODAY

The floodtide of the Japanese invasion that swept across southern Burma and then surged inland up the wide valleys of the Irrawaddy and Salween rivers to Mandalay and beyond between January and May 1942 has left comparatively few traces. A combination of the passage of time and the extensive post-war development of Burmese cities, towns and villages has transformed the countryside in southern and central Burma and swallowed up many of the few vestiges this short campaign left behind.

Scattered traces of the fighting during the Retreat from Burma can be found by a very careful observer. Some of the colonial-era buildings damaged during Japanese air raids on Rangoon still bear some scars of the war. It is still possible to stand on the eastern ridge above Moulmein, for example, and pick out the defensive perimeter used during the short-lived defence of the town. A few reminders of the hard-fought stand at the Bilin River line can also be found in the outline of old defensive positions hidden amidst the fast-growing tropical vegetation. The massive, solid concrete piers of the railway bridge across the Sittang River, clearly visible from Pagoda Hill where such desperate fighting took place in February 1942, still poke their heads above the fast-flowing river that claimed so many lives, although the bridge itself has been replaced by another built close nearby.

Many of the burial sites of the dead still remain, with others remembered on memorials. A large memorial and wall relief in the grounds of the Hote Wan Temple at Toungoo stands in silent testimony to the dead of the 200th Division and Chinese Expeditionary Force in general, while small cemeteries scattered over northern Burma contain the bodies of Nationalist Chinese servicemen who died in 1942.

Perhaps the single greatest visible reminder of the Japanese invasion and ensuing bitter fighting is the immaculate Taukkyan War Cemetery, maintained by the Commonwealth War Graves Commission. It contains the mortal remains of British, Indian and Burmese soldiers who paid the ultimate price in battle, died of wounds or else succumbed to tropical disease. This poignant burial ground – 21 miles north from the centre of Rangoon in the township of Mingaladon – contains the graves of 6,734 British Commonwealth servicemen who died in Burma during World War II, including those who fell in 1942. Within its grounds, the Rangoon Memorial records the names of almost 27,000 men whose final resting place is unknown. The separate Taukkyan Memorial also commemorates the names of 46 servicemen from both World War I and World War II who are buried elsewhere in Burma whose graves could not be physically maintained.

The poignant grave marker here in Taukkyan Cemetery, built and maintained by the Commonwealth War Graves Commission, marks the final resting place of an unknown British soldier who died while serving in Burma between 1942 and 1945. (mohigan, CC BY-SA 3.0)

Finally, the Taukkyan Cremation Memorial commemorates more than 1,000 soldiers who bodies were burned in accordance with their religious beliefs.

ACRONYMS AND ABBREVIATIONS

ABDACOM	Australian, British, Dutch and American Command		GSOII	General Staff Officer Grade II
			GSOIII	General Staff Officer Grade III
AHQ	Army Headquarters		HQ	headquarters
AVG	American Volunteer Group		IJA	Imperial Japanese Army
BFF	Burma Frontier Force		KOYLI	King's Own Yorkshire Light Infantry
BIA	Burma Independence Army		LMG	light machine gun
BMP	Burma Military Police		MC	Military Cross
C-in-C	Commander in Chief		MG	machine gun
CEF	Chinese Expeditionary Force		MMG	medium machine gun
CO	Commanding Officer		OC	Officer Commanding
DSO	Distinguished Service Order		RAF	Royal Air Force
GHQ	General Headquarters		RE	Royal Engineers
GOC	General Officer Commanding		RN	Royal Navy
GOC in C	General Officer Commanding in Chief		SMG	sub-machine gun
GSOI	General Staff Officer Grade I			

SELECT BIBLIOGRAPHY

Allen, Louis, *Burma: The Longest War 1941–45* (London: J.M. Dent, 1984)

Bond, Brian and Tachikawa, Kyoichi (eds), *British and Japanese Military Leadership in the Far Eastern War, 1941–1945* (London: Frank Cass, 2004)

Carew, Tim, *The Longest Retreat: The Burma Campaign 1942* (London: Hamish Hamilton, 1969)

Draper, Alfred, *Dawns Like Thunder: The Retreat from Burma* (London: Pen & Sword, 1987)

Grant, Ian Lyall and Tamayama, Kazuo, *Burma 1942: The Japanese Invasion* (London: Zampi, 1999)

Grehan, John and Mace, Martin, *The Fall of Burma 1941–43* (London: Pen & Sword Military, 2015)

Hedley, John, *Jungle Fighter: Infantry Officer, Chindit and SOE Agent in Burma* (London: Tom Donovan Publishing, 1996)

Jeffreys, Alan and Rose, Patrick (eds), *The Indian Army 1939–47* (Farnham: Ashgate, 2012)

Johnson, Rob, *The British Indian Army: Virtue and Necessity* (Newcastle upon Tyne: Scholars, 2014)

Kirby, Major-General S. Woodburn, *The War against Japan*, Volume II: *India's Most Dangerous Hour* (London: HMSO, 1958)

Lathrop, Alan K., 'The Employment of Chinese Nationalist Troops in the First Burma Campaign', *Journal of South-East Asian Studies*, Volume 12, No. 2 (September 1981), pp. 403–42

Leigh, Michael, *The Evacuation of Civilians from Burma: Analysing the 1942 Colonial Disaster* (London: Bloomsbury, 2014)

Li Chen, 'The Chinese Army in the First Burma Campaign', *Journal of Chinese Military History*, 2:1 (2013), pp.43–73

Lunt, James, *A Hell of a Licking: The Retreat from Burma 1941–42* (London: Harper Collins, 1986)

Lyman, Robert, *Slim, Master of War: Burma and the Birth of Modern Warfare* (London: Constable, 2004)

Lyman, Robert, *The Generals: From Retreat to Victory in Asia, 1941–45* (London: Constable, 2008)

Lyman, Robert, *Bill Slim* (Oxford: Osprey Publishing Ltd, 2011)

Mains, Lieutenant-Colonel Tony, *The Retreat from Burma: An Intelligence Officer's Personal Story* (London: Foulsham 1973)

Moreman, Tim, *The Jungle, the Japanese and the Commonwealth Armies at War 1941–45* (London: Frank Cass, 2005)

Nicholls, C.G., *Blow the Bridge: Fighting the Japanese in Burma* (London: Pen Press Publishers, 2005)

Prasad, Bisheshwar (ed.), *The Retreat from Burma 1941–45* (New Delhi: Combined Inter-Services Historical Section, 1954)

Preston-Hough, Peter, *Commanding Far Eastern Skies: A Critical Analysis of the Royal Air Force Air Superiority Campaign in India, Burma and Malaya 1941–1945* (London: Helion, 2015)

Roy, Kaushik, *Sepoys against the Rising Sun: The Indian Army in Far East and South-East Asia 1941–1945* (Leiden: Brill, 2015)

Slim, Field Marshal Sir William, *Defeat into Victory* (London: Cassell, 1952)

Smith, E.D., *The Battle for Burma* (London: Batsford, 1979)

Warren, Alan, *Burma 1942: The Road from Rangoon to Mandalay* (London: Continuum, 2011)

Woods, Philip, 'Filming the Retreat from Burma, 1942: British Newsreel Coverage of the Longest retreat in British Army History', *Historical Journal of Film, Radio and Television*, 35:3 (2015), pp. 438–53

Woods, Philip, *Reporting the Retreat: War Correspondents in Burma* (London: Hurst, 2016)